THE INSTITUTE FOR NATIONAL STRATEGIC STUDIES

MILITARY IMPLICATIONS OF

UNITED NATIONS

PEACEKEEPING OPERATIONS

Edited by William H. Lewis

NATIONAL DEFENSE UNIVERSITY

McNair Paper Seventeen

June 1993

For sale by the U.S. Government Printing Office
Superintendent of Documents, Mail Stop: SSOP, Washington, DC 20402-9328
ISBN 0-16-041972-7

NATIONAL DEFENSE UNIVERSITY ☐ *President:* Lieutenant General Paul G. Cerjan ☐ *Vice President*: Ambassador Howard K. Walker **INSTITUTE FOR NATIONAL STRATEGIC STUDIES** ☐ *Director:* Stuart E. Johnson

Publications Directorate ☐ Fort Lesley J. McNair ☐ Washington, D.C. 20319–6000 ☐ Phone: (202) 475–1913 ☐ Fax: (202) 475–1012 ☐ *Director:* Frederick T. Kiley ☐*Deputy Director:* Lieutenant Colonel Barry McQueen ☐ Chief, Publications Branch: George C. Maerz ☐ *Editors:* Kathleen A. Lynch and Mary A. Sommerville ☐ *Secretary:* Laura Hall ☐ *Circulation Manager:* Myrna Morgan

Cover Design: Juan A. Medrano #28406768

William H. Lewis is a Professor, The Elliott School, George Washington University. Previously, he was a Senior Fellow, Institute for National Strategic Studies, National Defense University.

From time to time, INSS publishes short papers to provoke thought and inform discussion on issues of U.S. national security in the post–Cold War era. These monographs present current topics related to national security strategy and policy, defense resource management, international affairs, civil-military relations, military technology, and joint, combined, and coalition operations.

Opinions, conclusions, and recommendations, expressed or implied, are those of the authors. They do not necessarily reflect the views of the National Defense University, the Department of Defense, or any other U.S. Government agency.

Readers are invited to submit (nonreturnable) manuscripts for consideration for publication. Please submit them in WordPerfect 5.1 on 3.5 inch diskettes with one printout.

Contents

MILITARY IMPLICATIONS OF

UNITED NATIONS

PEACEKEEPING OPERATIONS

PEACE-KEEPING FORCES AND OBSERVER MISSIONS

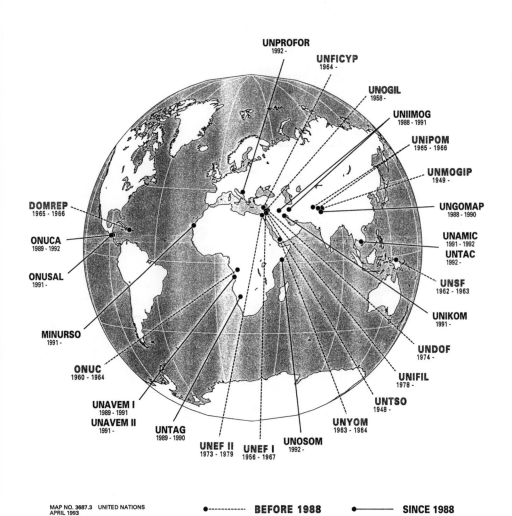

UNPROFOR
1992 -

UNFICYP
1964 -

UNOGIL
1958 -

UNIIMOG
1988 - 1991

UNIPOM
1965 - 1966

UNMOGIP
1949 -

UNGOMAP
1988 - 1990

UNAMIC
1991 - 1992

UNTAC
1992 -

UNSF
1962 - 1963

UNIKOM
1991 -

UNDOF
1974 -

UNIFIL
1978 -

UNTSO
1948 -

UNYOM
1963 - 1964

UNOSOM
1992 -

UNEF I
1956 - 1967

UNEF II
1973 - 1979

UNTAG
1989 - 1990

UNAVEM II
1991 -

UNAVEM I
1989 - 1991

ONUC
1960 - 1964

MINURSO
1991 -

ONUSAL
1991 -

ONUCA
1989 - 1992

DOMREP
1965 - 1966

MAP NO. 3687.3   UNITED NATIONS
APRIL 1993

● - - - - - - - - - -   **BEFORE 1988**   ● ──────── **SINCE 1988**

Introduction

by

Dr. William H. Lewis
George Washington University

THE ACTIONS BY THE UNITED NATIONS Security Council in the matter of Iraq's attempt to annex Kuwait have lead some observers to conclude that the United Nations is now well positioned to play a consequential role in the maintenance of international order. The coalition formed to meet Iraq's aggression included thirty-seven member states from five continents. This successful action represented a significant precedent for future preventive diplomacy and collective security actions by the world body. As one senior Canadian official somewhat exuberantly observed, a powerful message has been sent: "the United Nations, can as it was intended, safeguard world order and security."

The organization had been playing a stellar role in the cause of peace for a number of years. Prior to the 1990-91 Gulf War, the United Nations had been accorded recognition for its contributions to peace and stability. In September 1988, the Nobel Peace Prize was awarded for the organization's efforts in the field. At the time of the award, observer forces were in Afghanistan and Pakistan monitoring Soviet troop withdrawals from Afghanistan; 350 men were on duty in the Gulf to serve as a buffer between Iraq and Iran in compliance with a United Nations cease-fire resolution; concomitantly, the Secretary-General was organizing a peacekeeping unit for deployment to

Namibia, and was preparing for future involvement in conflicts in the Western Sahara, Kampuchea, and Central America.

The invasion of Kuwait by the forces of Saddam Hussein on August 2, 1990 was a qualitatively different situation, however. As President Bush noted, it represented the first major crisis to confront the international community in the post-Cold War period. The crisis would ultimately require the organization of massive military efforts to force the expulsion of Iraqi forces from Kuwait.

Even more critically, in the wake of the war, the Security Council took several punitive actions against Iraq that could serve as precedent in dealing with future acts of aggression. Most notable:

- ▸ Creation of a special agency to monitor the destruction of Iraq's chemical, biological and nuclear weapons;
- ▸ Determination of the circumstances and the conditions under which Iraq may export its oil and related products; and
- ▸ Deployment of monitors to ensure humanitarian treatment by Baghdad of its Kurdish and Shiite communities.

These were more than onerous cease-fire conditions; rather, they signalled the Security Council's determination to penalize the Iraqi regime with terms that were the political and legal equivalent of the Versailles Treaty. On the other hand, the mood of high expectation regarding future United Nations performance in the cause of peace encountered in the United States was not widely shared by other member states. The new-found unity among the permanent members of the Security Council has been greeted with ambivalence by others, many feeling themselves threatened by American "hegemony" or potentially marginalized by the "Big Five."

To address these developments and their implications for the US military, the Institute for National Strategic Studies of the National Defense University organized a series of conferences and special seminars, beginning in October 1991. The meetings brought together an outstanding group of senior officials, officers of flag rank, and national security policy specialists. The most recent meeting in the series–a one-day seminar convened on November 17, 1992–assessed problems confronted by United Nations military leaders as they engaged in peacekeeping missions. Their observations, frequently candid, provide useful insights regarding problems of effective command and control.

To make the results of these meetings available to a wider audience, we are re-publishing the previously published proceedings as a McNair Paper. In this new edition, we've added the keynote address by Ambassador Thomas R. Pickering, then United States Permanent Representative to the United Nations, given at the opening conference held on October 9, 1991. This addendum is particularly valuable given the current difficult policy issues and choices confronting the US Government in the field of international peacekeeping and conflict resolution.

Military Implications of United Nations Peacekeeping Operations

Ambassador Howard Walker
Vice President, NDU

IT IS MY GREAT PLEASURE on behalf of General Cerjan, the President of the University, to welcome you to this third in a series of workshops sponsored by the National Defense University's Institute for National Strategic Studies on "Future Security Roles of the United Nations." Since our last workshop on this subject in September when Ambassador and former UN Under Secretary, Ron Spiers, talked to us, interest in that subject has grown in the US, partly as a result of President Bush's speech at the United Nations in which he committed the United States to increased support for UN peacekeeping. Interest has grown at a time when the consequences of UN peacekeeping have exploded in cost and in complexity of operation. We see in Bosnia and Somalia today civil wars that are brutal and that are difficult to control. Injecting UN peacekeeping operations into those situations has far-reaching human and material costs. Equally important for us at this time in our history and for other countries, intervention has uncertain consequences and outcomes that affect the willingness of some governments and their citizens to participate. That makes it all the more important that we understand as fully as we can the nature of peacekeeping operations and the consequences for the US of military involvement.

We are very fortunate to have with us today to lead the discussion on this subject two gentlemen with impressive credentials.

Mr. Richard M. Connaughton was educated at Duke of York's Royal Military School, at Sandhurst, and at St. John's College at Cambridge University where he took a Master of Philosophy Degree in International Relations, and was also a Defense Fellow. He was commissioned in the Royal Armed Service Corps in 1961 and spent seven years in the Far East seconded to the Brigade of Ghurkas. He commanded squadrons and regiments in Germany, thereafter served as instructor at the British and Australian Army Command and Staff Colleges. He was head of the British Army's defense studies program. He retired as colonel two months ago and is currently working as a consultant in the field of national and international relations. Mr. Connaughton is the author of a number of publications on the subject of military security.

The other panelist is Mr. John Mackinlay who is senior research associate at the Thomas J. Watson Institute for International Studies at Brown University. After finishing Sandhurst, he joined the army in 1964 and retired a year ago. He developed his interest in international military cooperation while on the staff of the commander of the Multinational Force and Observers in the Sinai. He was the author of The Peacekeepers, an assessment of peacekeeping operations at the Arab-Israeli interface which compares UN and non-UN peacekeeping operations from both military and political points of view. He is currently researching new guidelines for multilateral military operations in the post Cold-War era. This Ford Foundation project, which Mr. Mackinlay directs, is entitled: "Second Generation Multinational Forces."

Command, Control and Coalition Operations

Richard M. Connaughton

MY TASK IS TO DISCUSS ASPECTS of Command, Control and Coalition Operations. Coalition Operations as a plausible means of collective security is a fact of life. Whereas responsible states are unlikely to declare unequivocally their eschewing of unilateral military action, the interplay of economic and political ramifications alone would indicate that multilateral military action will be the norm for the future. In the ending of the Cold War we have rediscovered the possibility of employing military power as a positive instrument of foreign policy. This paper is deliberately directed at UN-type operations rather than at multilateral ad hoc arrangements.

I have often thought that the coupling of Control to Command — and here I mean it in its military sense — implies a parity between the two functions. It suits my purpose today to contest that assumption. Command concerns the direction, coordination and control of military forces. Control is therefore but an adjunct to the function of command; it is impossible to command successfully without exercising control. Control is essentially a mechanism through which the commander, assisted by his staff, directs, organises and co-ordinates those forces for which he is responsible. I propose to concentrate this short study upon multilateral military command.

The other side of the Command and Control coin is the political face. But here the relative importance between the two functions is the reverse to that seen in the military dimension. Political command is essentially an American phenomenon, therefore being a national rather than multinational consideration. That is not to say the exercise of national command has no international implications. The great grey area which warrants serious study is the political control of military coalition operations.

Our topic has been finessed to examine military command and political control of coalition operations. The five parameters elected to form the basis for this short analysis and future discussion are:

> ►An Historical Perspective.
> ►The Relationship between Peacekeeping and Peace Enforcement.
> ► Command and the Commander.
> ► The Essence of Decision-Making in Coalition Operations.
> ► A Politico-Military Interface for the Future.

AN HISTORICAL PERSPECTIVE

If we had seen the end of history, what is happening out there in the world today must be something of a revival. Coalition or Alliance warfare has been a recurring feature of past conflicts. Perhaps I should add that a coalition differs from an alliance principally in degree; the latter tends to be more formal and longer lasting. The great 'British' victory of 1815 over the French at Waterloo was achieved by Wellington with only thirty-eight percent of his force originating from the British Isles.

In the previous century, Winston Churchill's ancestor, the Duke of Marlborough, rarely recruited more than a quarter of his army from Britain. In those days it was traditional to hire troops from the minor states of Europe for a campaigning season which fitted in between the Spring and Autumn. Successful generals were invariably successful diplomats as well as being politically astute. Marlborough was a past master in the manipulation of the kings and princes of Europe as well as controlling and commanding his representative foreign generals. It was no easy task, requiring exhaustive diplomacy. In the close season, he worked with the political committees in London to ensure that he would want for nothing when the improving weather presaged the resumption of hostilities. As ever, good quality intelligence was a primary consideration. Marlborough had succeeded in obtaining the services of a spy within Louis XIV's inner circle — le Conseil d'en Haute, an all-informed group of no more than a dozen of France's most influential courtiers and diplomats. The existence of the Versailles mole is a reminder to us of the importance of so-called human intelligence and that inadequacies here will undermine the effectiveness of the military operation.

The problem is that generals of Marlborough's quality only appear once or twice in a century. What we must studiously avoid is the recommendation and putting in place of a structure which only a Marlborough can make work.

So we can tick off a number of enduring prerequisites, as important today as they were then. Perhaps what we should be asking ourselves is, what weight should we attach to historical example? We have to understand that history does not really repeat itself. There will be similarities between events, but those will be balanced by dissimilarities. It is too simplistic to assert that coalitions are not new, without pausing to acknowledge that the circumstances in which they took place in the past were invariably different from today. A state of war would usually have existed, there were probably agreed missions, agreed preliminary plans, a known enemy and specified objectives. What history does is to provide us with the challenge of achieving as many of the above objectives as possible through abstract peacetime planning.

There is an important role for historians to play in the decision-making process. The aforementioned revival of history will serve to emphasize that ethnic, religious and national groups' behavior will often have a rationale rooted deep in their past. History is an arrow in the quiver of appraisal. One part of that balanced appraisal is to divorce ourselves from our western preconceptions, to step into the shoes of those whom we need to comprehend, and to observe the world from where they stand.

THE RELATIONSHIP BETWEEN PEACEKEEPING AND PEACE ENFORCEMENT

Normally, a few definitions would be in order, but I fear that this is an area notoriously difficult to define. In his paper Agenda for Peace, the UN Secretary-General, Dr. Boutros-Ghali made a rare attempt, for one within the UN, to define peacekeeping and its associated activities. Unfortunately, the result has been to further cloud the issue. So much so, for example, that the term 'peacemaking' has been rendered so ambiguous that it is recommended that its use be discontinued. To be fair, many of today's UN peace-inspired operations are resisting template categorization and this is a trend which will continue to be a feature of the future. The safest ploy is to adopt a functional approach to the peace-associated business.

The first function is Peace Enforcement, or Military Intervention. The victorious allies who had crafted and unveiled the Charter of the United Nations in 1945 had made a conscious effort in Chapter VII of the Charter to address the principal weakness of the Covenant of the League of Nations--the absence of an enforcement mechanism with which to defeat aggression. However, their subsequent conduct emphasized the point that these had been nations united in war against a common enemy. With the enemy defeated, there was no longer a bonding agent. Competing ideologies developed, and east and west went their separate ways. With them went the prospect of achieving a collective enforcement regime, frozen out by the Cold War.

Instead, and over a period of time, there emerged something not provided for within the Charter and our second function, traditional peacekeeping. The fundamental difference between the enforcement/intervention and peacekeeping functions has been described by Alan James:

> Yet when compared with military intervention, there is a distinction between the two (which) was seen to lie in their attitudes towards the associated issues of force and consent, collective security relying, ultimately on the mandatory use of force, while peacekeeping eschewed force, except in self-defense, and required the consent of the host state for the admission of UN personnel.

For convenience, peacekeeping settled comfortably under the umbrella of Chapter VI of the UN Charter, The Pacific Settlement of Disputes. Peacekeeping developed into the field of specialism of what tended to be the smaller and non-aligned states.

Strangely, only in the Congo, 1961-63, has the understanding that weapons are to be used purely in self-defense been comprehensively prejudiced. However, we are undoubtedly moving towards an uncertain, more violent future where the lightly trained but willing conscript will prove unequal to the task. We have the evidence of the limitations of conscripts from conflicts in Vietnam and Afghanistan. Recently, the Finnish commander at UNIFIL, General Hägglünd, stressed that the concept of enforcing peace should not be opposed:

> ...it simply requires different forces and a completely different concept. An intention to deter and enforce require forces which are as frightening as possible. For this kind of mission great-power battalions, professional soldiers and all the means at their disposal are preferable.

The combatants in the target country will frankly not be impressed by the security guarantees offered by those whom they consider to be militarily inferior. This is not to say that traditional peacekeeping should not continue where it can function. New problems demand new solutions. One new solution is the concept of preventive deployment. Here, the use of force, if necessary, is implicit. This is therefore our third function, what I will describe as aggravated peacekeeping, lying somewhere between Chapters VI and VII and what Dag Hammarskjold appropriately described as Chapter VI½.

The European coalition operation in Bosnia is not intervention, nor what is accepted as traditional peacekeeping. It is a new category of humanitarian activity mounted with, in theory, the permission of the parties involved. The force's response to aimed fire will be less passive than what has prevailed in the past. It is for this reason that it has the potential to fall within the ambit of Chapter VI½.

What the Yugoslavia crisis has done has been to beg serious questions of the *modus operandi*, and to expose a number of the negative aspects of the UN. The Organization has found itself overstretched and, in the case of Bosnia, unable to mount a major military operation. The procedure whereby headquarters and forces are assembled on the principle of equitability, geographical distribution and providing for the employment of up to one-third women, has clearly been found wanting. But, in the past, the UN has got by, its skimpy military staff relying upon the *ad hoc* hot plan, supported by what Sir Brian Urquhart has described as a cobbled together 'Sheriff's Posse.'

Major military players will expect as a minimum for their own troops, the presence of a robust, coherent and practised centre core headquarters. Chapter VI½ and Chapter VII-scale operations cannot be commanded or controlled without a proper military structure. Since the European Community is paying the Bosnian UNPROFOR 2 'peacekeeping' bill, they have their way, but soon the strained civil-military relationship within the UN will have to be addressed.

In the first 40 years of the UN's life, it undertook 13 peacekeeping operations. In the four years from 1988, it has equalled that total. It is not simply the evaporation of ideological sparring which has prompted the exponential increase in UN peacekeeping activity. It is also a reflection of changing international attitudes. For example, it was a sovereign right that states were free to act as they chose within the confines of their own borders. When opprobrious behaviour was challenged by other states, Article 2(7) of the UN Charter was employed as the authority to continue to behave badly. The effectiveness of Article 2(7) first began to erode in relation to South Africa in the 1960s. That it has lost much of its psychotic sanctity was apparent in 1991 when 20,000 NATO troops were deployed into northern Iraq without Iraq's consent and without significant protest from world opinion. It would seem that if care is taken in the presentation of cases for legitimate military intervention — they will invariably be in support of regional actors — then it need not be seen within the UN's General Assembly as a colonial imposition. It is unfortunate that there does appear to be a continuing need to remind the major actor that the authority for military action has its source of origin in New York and not in Washington.

Understandably, the increase in both UN commitments and the nature of some of those commitments will be reflected in a greater demand for professional forces, particularly logisticians. Those forces will be called upon to intervene in the conventional fighting which is a feature of inter-state conflict and the 'brutal, ethnic, religious, social, cultural or linguistic strife' described by Dr. Boutros-Ghali as the unconventional features apparent in intra-state conflict. There will be difficulties in presentation, and reserves of diplomacy will be taxed, but if the old order of states is to be employed to face the new order's disorder, then it requires headroom within the UN for essential contingency planning. We should set aside our unreasonable sensitivity in involving the Military Staff Committee in the planning process and follow the lead taken by the Western European Union. Diplomacy has to release more responsibility and authority to the military. The fact of the matter is that, while soldiers can be diplomats, diplomats cannot be soldiers.

COMMAND AND THE COMMANDER

Command of a coalition operation will be vested in the nominated commander from either a framework state or security organization. The framework state will often be the major investor in the enterprise, the state normally providing the largest national military contribution, a large proportion of the infrastructure support, and a significant percentage of the operation's costs. I have in mind here a deployed US Unified Command and, for convenience, will describe this as the Unified Command Model. There is some attraction in relating the United States to this model, but these models are by nature general rather than specific. We should not assume either that the USA will always be the dominant player or that the USA template is entirely appropriate to other framework states.

The military commander is the key ingredient in the working of an effective coalition. The award of high command cannot be tempered by charity, by the concept of Buggins's turn, for every headquarters with the remotest prospect of leading an international military operation requires at the apex of its pyramid the right man at the right time. If coalitions are to survive internal and external political/military pressure and tensions, the hope will be that they are of short duration. In the world wars there was time to test the many generals who had risen to command positions as peacetime trainers and administrators. Those who did not succeed were removed. Coalitions will not enjoy this validatory period. Moreover, there are practical difficulties in having a general removed who is not one of your own nationals, so it is more than likely that the military commander who embarks upon the operation will, for better or for worse, be there at the end.

It seems that the modern coalition commander requires a minimum of four basic qualities; he has to be adept in the skills

of operational decision-making, the science of management, the
art of leadership, and to possess the gift of intellect. These
qualities are of course a permutation of attributes which go back
in history. 'Management' is akin to control and it can be taken
to mean control, but there is a subtle difference which can be
illustrated with reference to the question of media relations. The
commander, through his staff, will manage those members of the
press corps amenable to such management, and will control those
who are not.   But the one quality of the moment is that of
intellect. It is today's prerequisite. Its absence will filter out
those who in the past would have climbed the ladder of success
through undoubted qualities of confidence, charisma and natural
leadership. If a future coalition commander lacks intellect, he
will be unable to hold his own in a highly charged political and
diplomatic environment, his essential media image will be
impaired and he is unlikely to be able to comprehend the abiding
human aspects in dealing with and tasking with equanimity a
multiplicity of national representatives - all with their own
national, political points to score and careers to enhance. And all
this before we consider the enemy!

Effective command can best be achieved through a formed
headquarters with a proven track record.   The nominated
commander's own joint staff are practised in playing a full part
in the success, or failure, of their commander's plans. They are
a team which it is difficult to conceive can be improved by the
introduction within the core of additional, token, representative
staff officers. I am not referring here to liaison officers. Liaison
officers should, as a matter of routine, already be in place in any
headquarters liable to be earmarked to command coalition
operations.   The commander and his staff have the benefit of
knowing one another, their strengths and weaknesses, and should
have developed an effective working relationship.   One
instinctively senses when the atmosphere in a headquarters is
right, aware that internal and external pressures will be addressed
with quiet confidence and that the staff's entire energy is
dedicated to the support of their commander. All this is, of
course, to talk of the ideal. Compromise will be the rule rather
than the exception.

If, therefore, I am suggesting that the commander and his
own Joint Headquarters Staff, or what we shall call the Combined

Task Force Headquarters (CTFHQ), are an indivisible entity, what should be the relationship between the commander and the subordinate, national military representatives (MILREPS)? The analogy I shall use in illustrating the Unified Command Model is that of a galaxy of national, non-operational headquarters whose relative position to CTFHQ is indicative of their importance to the operation. In support of the framework state will be a secondary state. The relationship between the framework state and the secondary state will be determined by a number of factors which can be collectively described as 'empathy.' The function of the secondary state is no sinecure. It is essentially the coalition's Union representative, the one voice and opinion the Commander must find the time to consider. Above all, the commander of the secondary state's forces must ensure that the relationship between the framework state and the other supporting states remains that of allies, not as a grouping of auxiliaries. The secondary state's national headquarters in our hypothetical galaxy is the closest to the core headquarters. Indeed, in the Gulf, the British MILREP was invited into General Schwarzkopf's CTFHQ.

Time marches on, but I think it useful to put down a number of bullets to describe the command relationship between CTFHQ and the national staffs:

▷ CTFHQ and national staffs remain rigorously distinct.

▷ The commander is advised to conduct separate, bilateral discussions on specific issues with his constellation of national commanders. It is most important that the national commanders do have the opportunity to reinforce what they feel their capitals want, as well as convey their own personal thoughts. If the commander consults his allies individually rather than en masse (time permitting), he avoids competition for his ears, he can detect problems, nervousness, and sense political complications. What has to be studiously avoided during this dialogue is the generation of a sense of favouritism, suspicion and conspiracy. When the round is complete, the commander directs his staff to design what is in effect a collaborated plan which is then presented by the

CTFHQ staff to the assembled national commanders. The commander, therefore, has the benefit of knowing the answers to questions which might arise and is also conscious that he is not presenting proposals which are unacceptable to the national commanders.

▷ There are advantages in the subordinate Joint Task Force Headquarters (JTFHQ) being formed and commanded by representatives of the framework state. It is self-evident that the framework state should also be responsible for the tools of command — e.g., communications.

There is a further model which I shall describe as the NATO Model. This ·model refers to an existing international headquarters, but one with its won integral, political, regulatory council. An obvious example is the Allied Command Europe Rapid Reaction Corps (ACERRC). The headquarters sent into Bosnia to command British, Canadian, Spanish and French battalion groups on Operation UNPROFOR II is a subordinate, debaptised NATO headquarters. The variation on the theme is obviously necessary due to French participation, particularly the nomination of Major General Phillipe Morillon to command the force.

I am not proposing an embryonic UN Headquarters Model because I feel it would be unworkable in practice. It is not so much the beguiling influence of the UN's composition rules but rather the reality that, on occasions, constituent members would be debarred from participating due to a conflict of national interest. Crises will never be the same. The solution may well lie in a menu of on-call, formed national or international headquarters, called forward to command the operation based upon that headquarter's suitability.

THE ESSENCE OF DECISION-MAKING IN COALITION OPERATIONS

I shall not dwell on this subject, but it does require discussion in order to construct a foundation for the finale.

It is crises which spawn coalitions. Coalitions will rarely be formed entirely from one of the myriad, regional, collective security organisations. There are two principal, positive[1] reasons for states to throw their hat into the coalition ring. Either the crisis impinges upon a vital national interest, or the state sees it as its international responsibility to act. Coalitions can only be held together when there is unity of purpose, an unequivocal aim, and an agreed mission statement. A flaw was apparent in the decision-making process during Operation Provide Comfort, alias Haven, a 1991 humanitarian operation aimed at providing relief to Iraq's Kurds. In this case, the responsible Unified Command was US EUCOM, supported by contingents made available from other states. EUCOM, however, had a national mission:

> Combined Task Force Provide Comfort conducts multinational humanitarian operations to provide relief to displaced Iraqi civilians until International Relief arrives.

Indeed, EUCOM's commander, General Shalikashvili, was the Command's deputy who, despite commanding an international operation, received his orders from his national headquarters. In the House of Commons, Prime Minister John Major emphasised that without suitable assurances on the safety of Iraq's Kurds, British troops would not be withdrawn. It was not operationally possible for British troops to remain in Northern Iraq without the support of American forces. However, there was a crucial disparity between General Shalikashivili's mission statement and the conditions John Major deemed to be necessary before British forces were to be withdrawn:

> ...firstly, an effective UN force on the ground; secondly, clear warnings to Iraq that any renewed repression will meet the severest response; thirdly, a continuing deterrent military presence in the region to back up those warnings, and the maintenance of sanctions against Iraq. Without those we will not leave.

But the American Supreme Commander, his mission statement having been satisfied, had begun the initial, partial withdrawal from Northern Iraq. The timing was unfortunate because it served to undermine the Kurdish leaders' negotiating position with Iraq. The point is obvious. The decision-making process is influenced by domestic and external factors which have to be collaborated into coalition aims and mission statements. The success of future coalition operations should not be dependent upon ministers communicating informally with their coalition partners on an ad hoc, one-to-one basis. We are in danger of being lulled into a false sense of security. Coalitions will not always be as straightforward as those seen in the Gulf and in Northern Iraq. In both cases, the adequate though loose command and control relationships were not severely tested.

A POLITICO-MILITARY INTERFACE
FOR THE FUTURE

It appears to be an acceptable practice to excuse discordance within a coalition as the inevitable manifestation of political decisions being made at different times in different places. If such a state of affairs is not addressed, then Unified Command Model Operations are destined to continue in the manner of the worst case UN federal peacekeeping operation. We shall continue to observe national defense ministers with 'hands on' aspiration, directing their own national formations, sometimes unbeknown to the commanders.[2] We shall see rank inflation whereby the seniority of the senior representative of national teams exceeds what is justified. Such is the perfidy of national maneuvering in anticipation of achieving an unjustified position closer to or at the coalition high table. There can be little argument that there has to be a structure through which collaborated and singular, political control can be exercised. Foreign political leaders are reassured when they can see that adequate political control has been imposed upon a commander who is not of their nationality. In addition, the apparent collectivisation of the decision-making process has presentational advantages. The resultant military action is identified not with the administration organisation or collective defense agreement which mandates the essential authority to the military coalition.

The singular line of political direction to the coalition commander will represent a distillation of the views of the national representatives within the coalition. If we adopt a NATO-style organization and apply its principles to such *ad hoc* coalitions which emerge in the future then, in theory at least, the politicians will have a forum from which to exert control, leaving the commander free to command, unshackled from past, petty, political distractions. Constituent coalition members will be represented at ambassadorial level, convened centrally yet at some distance from the conflict.

The line diagram would look something like this:

▸ *C² in Coalition Operations*

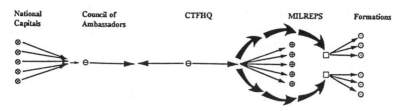

The line between the Council of Ambassadors to CTFHQ is not a one-way street. It is naive to believe that national capitals and coalition Ambassadors will not talk to their MILREP; indeed, for national decision-making as well as for routine and administrative matters such dialogue is essential. There may be reason and opportunity to collocate MILREPS with the Council of Ambassadors. The function of MILREP is firstly, to represent the national military interest, exercising the veto if required and, secondly, to maintain the Force in the Theatre including medical and personnel matters, national logistics and public relations. Operational discussions, however, must go through the chain of command. Similarly, national units within formations will wish to talk to their MILREPs, but this is not the route for operational decision-making. There must obviously be concern that the proposed Council might fail to reach agreement due to a conflict of national interests. However, the implications of political prevarication are such that the absence of a working structure such as the one described here, might result in the failure of the coalition's military mission.

CONCLUSION

We have an unusual situation whereby we have been discussing what is for us a new ball game, yet one for which we have not compiled the rules. We have barely acknowledged the necessity for purple planning before new horizons of political awareness and diplomatic liaison are demanding attention. Sooner, rather than later, most here will be drawn into the planning process, execution or conflict termination of UN or UN-mandated collective security initiatives. Coalitions involve compromise and a willingness to concede on issues of national sovereignty. When allied intransigence is at its most frustrating, it is as well to remember that we too are someone else's ally.

What is inescapable is the momentum driving the associated study of peace-associated military operations. It is all very well pointing to the somewhat obvious need for UN reform. The challenge lies in the formulation of acceptable procedures for the command and control of a new generation of peacekeeping and peace enforcement operations. What is more, procedures have to be practised. Politicians require to be persuaded of the need to raise the political profile, to play their part in coalition crisis management exercises, to acquaint themselves with options and likely areas where decisions will ultimately have to be made. What price WINTEX '94?

NOTES

1. Joining a coalition can also be for negative reasons, such as attempting to stop one coalition member dominating the operation, or preventing one set of outcomes.

2. National interference behind commanders' backs comes in a number of guises. It is useful to distinguish between micro-management during military operations (such as Carter in Tehran rescue bid) as distinct from political control over the identification of strategic objectives and interference as a consequence of domestic, public opinion regarding either methods used or casualties inflicted or received.

Defining A Role Beyond Peacekeeping

John Mackinlay

AFTER THE COMPARATIVE STABILITY of the Cold War, violence
is spreading contagiously through Yugoslavia and the multi-
ethnic states of the former Soviet Union. Rural and urban
communities have been torn apart by factional conflict and inter-
ethnic hatred, unleashing all the misery of massive population
displacement and its long term destabilizing effects.

Political disarray at NATO prevented an effective response
by the European nations and negative memories of the Soviet
empire inhibited a wider involvement by Russian forces.
Although the UN has to some extent been able to overcome the
political obstacles to an international response, it failed to
organize an effective multinational force which had the military
capabilities needed to police fragile agreements on the ground
and protect isolated minorities from the brutalities of local
factions. A similar lack of military effectiveness diminishes
chances of a successful outcome in Cambodia and Somalia. UN
planning staff in New York have once again applied the ad hoc
procedures used to assemble a peacekeeping force to situations
which demand a much more sophisticated approach. Although
"peacekeeping" relies on pre-conditions which are notably absent
in these contingencies, in each case UN troops arrived piecemeal,
in the planning expectation of a best case scenario.

This paper argues that the concept of peacekeeping as a
multipurpose conflict resolution device is already overextended
and cannot be adapted any further to meet the dynamic
contingencies of the future. In reality the UN peacekeepers have,
with mixed results, already crossed the threshold of traditional
peacekeeping operations into a new range of second generation
tasks. It is now time to spell out these tasks with greater
definition and develop an internationally agreed doctrine to
replace the ad hoc methods of the Cold War period.

LIMITATIONS OF THE PEACEKEEPING PROTOTYPE

United Nations peacekeeping developed as an instrument of a deeply divided Security Council during the Cold War. As a result there were important constraints in its application. The term "Peacekeeping" has no internationally authorized definition, not only because it does not appear in the UN Charter, but also because it has taken different forms to meet a number of different crises. It has also been misapplied outside the UN context to describe non UN multinational and unilateral interventions as well as UN operations which do not have any of the accepted characteristics of peacekeeping.

The UN refers to peacekeeping as "an operation involving military personnel, but without enforcement powers, undertaken by the United Nations to help maintain or restore international peace and security in areas of conflict." Under-Secretary-General for Peacekeeping Operations, Marrack Goulding, developed this definition:

> United Nation field operations in which international personnel, civilian and/or military, are deployed with the consent of the parties and under United Nations command to help control and resolve actual or potential international conflicts or internal conflicts which have a clear international dimension.

This definition and its related military concept of operations have been widely accepted among the major UN contingent contributing countries to describe the constrained, mainly interpositional, peacekeeping forces which were deployed during the period of the Cold War.

The principles of interpositional peacekeeping are derived from the regulations for the Second United Nations Emergency Force (UNEF 2) deployed to the Suez in the wake of the 1973 Arab-Israeli war. They were the product of previous UN experience and became the model for operations that followed. They gave guidance on:

    ▷ the need for support by the mandating authority, the Security Council;

    ▷ the requirement that the operation be deployed only with the consent of the warring parties;

▷ the command and control of the Force by the UN;

▷ the composition of the Force; the restriction that force be used only in self-defense; and

▷ the need for complete impartiality.

At all times, the Force had to have the full confidence and backing of the Security Council. In practice, this was not always forthcoming. A divided Security Council resulted in mandates which were sometimes based on a minimal area of common agreement. Often, following the deployment of a peacekeeping operation, no further adjustments could be made to the mandate and this reduced its effectiveness and credibility in the field and gave the appearance of weakness. Mandates tended to be restrictive in scope and sometimes vaguely expressed to avoid disagreement among the permanent members. As a result the peacekeepers' operational flexibility was reduced which limited their ability to adapt their role to the needs of a changing situation..Although the mutually agreed disinterest of the Security Council in the day to day conduct of operations gave peacekeepers impartiality in the Cold War scenario, it also removed from them the operational sophistication needed to meet changing situations with an effective military presence in the field.

UN peacekeeping forces tended to operate only with the full cooperation of the parties concerned. Peacekeepers did not have the military means to enforce a mandate from the Security Council. The consent and cooperation of the interested parties was therefore essential for success. This meant that a Force could only be deployed once the conflict began to stalemate or stabilize and a political will prevailed between the parties to seek an alternative to violence. Peacekeepers could not operate successfully until these conditions were met, particularly in the buffer zones where they supervised a strip of 'no-mans land,' which prior to their arrival was the site of an intense conflict between opposing, but easily identifiable, conventional forces.

According to the Secretary General's report (3) the "Force would be under the command of the United Nations, vested in the Secretary-General, under the authority of the Security Council. The command in the field would be exercised by a Force Commander appointed by the Secretary-General with the Council's consent. The Commander would be responsible to the

Secretary-General. The Secretary-General would keep the Security Council fully informed of developments relating to the functioning of the Force. All matters which could affect the nature or the continued effectiveness of the Force would be referred to the Council for its decision." This principle of command has largely remained intact.

The "Force would be composed of a number of contingents to be provided by selected countries, upon the request of the Secretary-General. The contingents would be selected in consultation with the Security Council and with the parties concerned, bearing in mind the accepted principle of equitable geographic representation." By tacit agreement this excluded permanent members of the Security Council from participating in peacekeeping operations, although there have been exceptions. Consequently, peacekeepers were drawn from middle level or small powers, some with only a limited military capability. The constrained and reactive tasks of peacekeeping did not demand more than this. In principle nations with small undeveloped military forces could, without threatening the parties involved, provide infantry units while nations with more sophisticated military powers provide the support units.

Peacekeepers would not use force except in self-defense. Self-defense would include resistance to attempts by forceful means to prevent it from discharging its duties under the Security Council's mandate. The definition of a defensive weapon was not explained which has left the choice open to manifold interpretations on a case by case basis. The rules of engagement also tended to vary from force to force and in some forces, particularly in the early phase of deployment, varied between contingents. But the significant factor is the constant assumption that the parties to the conflict would comply with the Council's decisions, which allowed UN military planners to assume a best case scenario at the outset of every operation. Once deployed, the UN peacekeepers tended to report on, but not intervene in, violent incidents or violations of peace agreements. Escalating the response beyond the use of force in self-defence was regarded as enforcement. Without the power or authority to take problem-solving action, except at a very local level, peacekeepers had to rely more on their symbolic international presence and the moral pressures arising from the disapproval of the international community.

In view of these limitations there was never much pressure on the UN planning staff to develop the capability to deploy or conduct an effective military operation. It is even possible that the largely civilian staff in the UN's Field Operations and External Support Activities Office did not appreciate what additional military planning skills were needed to meet a less than best case scenario. Although Force Commanders and individual staff officers published critical accounts of planning failures, particularly in the initial phases of deployment, there was no institutional process to capture these lessons and the same problems and mistakes occurred again at the initial phase of new forces. The strongest reason not to improve the system was the feeling in New York that, notwithstanding their short term discomforts and lack of effectiveness, the UN military presence was marginal to the success of the process.

POST COLD WAR DEVELOPMENTS

The end of the Cold War removed some of the political tensions in the UN that had limited the scope and application of peacekeeping. No longer subject to superpower confrontation and competition, the Security Council became increasingly effective with an enhanced ability to negotiate peace agreements in longstanding conflict zones. Peace forces were deployed with more explicit and firmly stated mandates than in the past. Changes also occurred in the longstanding indifference of the Security Council nations. The United States began to consider peacekeeping as a policy option, and has already taken steps in the Pentagon to plan for future involvement. The Soviet Union reversed its former cautious attitude which had inhibited the scope and conduct of some operations and earmarked armed forces for international peacekeeping roles. Both of these national shifts have opened the prospect of direct great power involvement in UN multinational forces.

But as the UN Security Council developed its sense of governance and began to address more challenging threats to security, the change from a bi-polar to a multi-polar global structure generated a new range of conflict. Problems that had been artificially stabilized in the bi-polar world were now exacerbated by the collapse of the Soviet Union. In addition to regional conflict, multi-ethnic states began to disintegrate and internal rather than inter-state conflicts proliferated. Humanitarian emergencies worsened and fragile governments emerged to fill the vacuum created by superpower withdrawals. The range of UN tasks had, de facto, been extended beyond the recognized limitations of "peacekeeping." In addition to the traditional roles of conventional observer missions and peacekeeping, UN forces were now involved in operations where the best case scenario could no longer be relied on: supervising cease-fires between irregular forces, assisting in the maintenance of law and order, protecting the delivery of humanitarian assistance, the denial of an air space and the guarantee of rights of passage. In many of these operations local factions would continue to resist the presence of UN troops in defiance of agreements made on their behalf in the distant environment of Geneva, Paris and London.

This surge in demand exhausted the capacity of the middle nations which habitually provided contingents, which included: Australia, Austria, Canada, Ireland, the Nordic countries, Poland and Fiji. Not only was there now a need to expand the pool of peacekeepers to include armies with more sophisticated assets, but also moral reasons why it was no longer acceptable for the major military powers to stand back and allow a group of smaller nations pay the price, in casualties as well as national resources, for their longstanding involvement in what should have been an international effort.[4]

Prior to the Gulf War, peace negotiating successes in the UN were already beginning to outstrip the willingness of members, and the capacity of the small secretariat staff, to provide and organize adequate multinational forces to supervise these new and complex agreements. Within the UN, member nations insisted on a ponderous system of authorization and funding that encumbered the launching of UN peace forces, to an extent that in some cases only leading elements could be made available at the critical early stages of a ceasefire.[5]

The widening gap between the UN's growing list of negotiated agreements and its ability to underwrite them with effective forces was revealed during the early stages of the Gulf confrontation. Although the UN had become the focal point at which the international community coalesced its support for some form of effective military action against Iraq. It soon became clear that there was no way in which the Security Council could direct or the UN Secretariat conduct a dynamic military campaign on the scale required. The collective membership, in some cases under pressure from the United States, had set aside their national and domestic interests to authorize the use of collective force under Security Council Resolution 678, but the coalition of forces that formed never seriously considered the idea of submitting themselves to a UN command. Whether or not this reluctance stemmed from a desire to impose a *pax americana* in the Gulf is outside the scope of this argument. The bare facts were that no vestiges of a command organization, not even a map room, existed in the UN which could direct the operations of an effective military force. Since the outset of the Cold War the UN had abandoned the development of any machinery to execute the enforcement measures of Chapter VII, and after years of neglect any residual military staff capability, as opposed to the organization of peacekeeping events, had long since turned to dust. Although "peacekeeping" forces continued to deploy to Namibia, Cambodia, Somalia and Croatia under the same planning assumptions as before, in reality there was now a much greater need for them to be militarily effective.

PROBLEMS FOR THE PEACEKEEPER

The absence of an effective response-doctrine for these new contingencies encouraged a new vocabulary, "peace-doing" epithets and buzzwords. These concealed a lack of any logically developed concept of military operations which could be appropriate to the rapidly changing situation. Words like "peace-making" and "peace-enforcement," used freely without any underlying doctrinal agreement as to what they meant, have developed opposite meanings in Brussels and in New York. Blurred by overexposure, the word "peacekeeping" had lost its former definition. In addition to its institutionally accepted meaning, it was now being used loosely to describe military activities which lay beyond its strictly defined UN parameters.

Hard and fast principles of consent were crumbling as new operations deployed to countries where a UN presence was evidently not universally accepted: to Croatia and Bosnia where armed local opposition from all parties resisted UN attempts to protect threatened communities, and to Cambodia where the armed forces of the Khmer Rouge refused to submit themselves to the cantonment processes of the Paris Agreement. In addition, greater use was being made of existing alliances. In May 1991, a Security Council authorized multinational force (Operation Safe Haven) flew into Northern Iraq against the wishes of Baghdad to assist and protect relief deliveries to the Kurds. In fall 1992, the Security Council authorized operations to deny the use of airspace by the Iraqis over Southern Iraq and in another resolution by the Bosnian Serbs around Sarajevo.

In June 1992, the UN Secretary-General issued a report entitled the "Agenda for Peace" outlining proposals for strengthening UN peace mechanisms. These included preventive measures, as well as a return to the original theme of the UN Charter in which agreements were negotiated that provided for armed forces to be available "on stand-by" for enforcement actions. In the short term the creation of "peace enforcement units" would allow the UN to respond to challenges beyond peacekeeping. The "Agenda for Peace" was the first step towards the development of a UN operational capability that could meet a second generation of new tasks. To be capable of exercising a wide range of military responses as situations escalate and deescalate, future operations would require the assets of major powers to enable a more a sophisticated range of response. These could be subordinated to an integrated command system.

On the ground at the violent interface these separate strands of development tended to place the peacekeeper (or more accurately the UN soldier) in a much more exposed position. He was still being deployed under the same ad hoc military staff procedures in which essential operational decisions were left to contingent level interpretation and the slow arrival or complete absence of logistic support in some theaters (for example initially in Somalia) prevented the establishment of an effective military presence. In the best case scenario it did not matter much, now it did.

The concept of peacekeeping in the widely accepted but rigid form of the traditional prototype cannot be adapted any further. An emerging era of multipolar international restructuring has brought with it a new range of operational tasks for the UN. These are no longer predicated on the logic of universal consent, and cannot safely assume the traditional scenario of an uncontested UN presence. They constitute a second generation of UN activities.

Second generation operations are already a fact of life. They fall between the techniques of peacekeepers and observers, and enforcement. The term "Second Generation" operations refers to a growing range of contingencies, sometimes incorrectly described as "peacekeeping" in which UN forces face an expanded range of tasks. These are distinct from peacekeeping because UN forces involved do not necessarily enjoy the support of all the parties involved locally and consequently will have to take much more rigorous steps to achieve a standard of military effectiveness that ensures their personnel safety and achieves the conditions required in the mandate. In some second generation tasks, authorized under an enforcement mandate, heavy weapons system including armored vehicles, combat aircraft and warships may be deployed.

SECOND GENERATION OPERATIONS

The rapidity of these developments has opened a doctrinal gap which is not covered by an international agreement. There is a procedural vacuum on how to translate the bare statements of a second generation mandate into a workable operational plan on the ground. In the Watson Institute project on Second Generation Multinational Operations we have found a growing consensus among NATO and national defense staff that the generic category of UN operations can now be more accurately sub-divided into nine distinct tasks. These can be explained in the form of a continuum starting with Observer Missions and Peacekeeping and escalating to Sanctions and High Intensity Operations. Below they have been arranged in three levels.

▷ **Level One** (Monitors and Supervision) comprises the well-defined tasks of observer missions and peacekeeping forces.

▷ **Level Two** (Reinforced Military Presence)describes five categories of operation which usually occur in conflict between communities within a state, rather than between states. Although UN multinational forces will be stronger and more effective, they will continue to operate under strict limitations of using the minimum amount of force required to achieve the immediate objective. This level is distinguished from Level One by the higher requirementor militarily effective contingents and the presence of some heavier weapon systems in the UN force.

▷ **Level Three** operations (Military Intervention) refer to enforcement operations where UN military forces with a substantial heavy weapons capability are used to redress a major threat to international peace and security. They are distinguished from Levels One and Two by the likelihood that incidents between UN forces and the sanctioned party are likely to occur at a very high level, typically between troops formations, combat aircraft or warships and not between small groups on the ground. Level Two operations are continuing to develop in their characteristics and scope. This is certainly the most dynamic area of UN operational activity.

There is unlikely to be a clearly defined boundary between each task. Within the authority of a single mandate a UN force may carry out several of the tasks defined below. Although the tasks in the continuum are shown in their likely order of operational intensity and the consequently increasing scale of UN commitment, this escalating order is not rigid. For example, it may be possible for a Level Two task to amount to a far larger and more intensive commitment than a Level Three sanction task.

Level One Operations

Observer Missions. A UN observer can be military or civilian, usually having the status of an officer, whose principle task is to observe and report on a developing situation, or on the execution of a peace agreement reached between conflicting parties.

Observers are usually unarmed; in some exceptional circumstances that may carry personal weapons. In addition to their supervisory and monitoring tasks observers may be deployed in a early warning role where a nation or ethnic group is seriously threatened by the aggressive actions of a neighboring party, in this case observers may be stationed at the mutual boundary or interface. Their task will be to provide timely and impartial information to the internal community through the UN of any threatening moves and developments. In some cases it may be necessary for the observers to act as a "trip wire" that is linked to a multinational deterrent force, lying outside the immediate area of tension which tacitly underwrites their presence.

Peacekeeping. A peacekeeping operation, as defined by the UN Secretariat and leading contributor nations, refers to the operations of multinational forces, usually authorized and organized under the auspices of the UN, to help maintain and restore international peace, without recourse to enforcement action. In relation to the parties in conflict peacekeeping forces are usually small and lightly armed. To be successful, they must rely on the consent of the parties and effectiveness of the political agreements which underwrite their presence and function in the peace process. They cannot rely on their military strength if the agreement breaks down, or a significant element of the opposed parties refuses to cooperate.

Level Two Operations

Preventive Deployment. Preventive deployment refers to the action by a UN multinational group or force at the interface or zone of potential conflict where tension is rising between parties. The use of preventive deployment does not rely first on a truce or peace plan having been agreed between the parties. Although UN contingents or observers will deploy with the consent or at the request of, one or all parties involved, it is unlikely that their specific task will have been agreed except in principle between parties. A preventive interpositional deployment may be organized from several national contingents on the same principle as a conventional peacekeeping force. Contingents may carry weapons necessary for protective tasks as well as self-defence.

The force will not be strong enough to resist a deliberate attack by one party or another, or restore territory unlawfully seized. Here the internal boundary or likely interface in dispute may be overrun in conflict. It is not, therefore, desirable to deploy UN assets which cannot be swiftly removed.

Internal Conflict Resolution Measures. These are the actions taken by a UN multinational force to restore and maintain an acceptable level of peace and personal security in an internal conflict. Their successful application relies first of all on a substantial level of local support for some form of conflict resolution to take place. UN forces involved in internal conflict resolution will be called on to provide a wide number of tasks that will vary considerably in each case. The following tasks are common to most situations:

- Provide Liaison between Parties
- Oversee Multi Party Ceasefire
- Cantonment
- Disarming
- Custody of War Supplies
- Supervising the Reconstitution of Host Nation Police and Defense Forces

Military Assistance to an Interim Civilian Authority. The provision of military assistance to an interim civil authority usually follows a successfully conducted ceasefire. Once a "safe" ceasefire has brought hostilities to a level which allows the resumption of civil order, the tempo of military activity will alter. The intense military activities related to the assembly and disarmament of the parties will move into a less dynamic phase in which the UN forces' military capability may be subordinated to the requirement of an interim civil authority. The overall task of the UN military force will be to supervise or police the provisions of a peace agreement and ensure the lead up to an election or transfer of power is conducted in a free and fair manner. UN forces involved in military assistance to an (interim) civil authority will be required to provide an extremely wide variety of support. The following tasks are common to most situations:

- Assist in the maintenance of law and order

▷ Assist in the provision of security prior to, and during, an election

▷ Help to maintain the smooth running of essential services (power, water, communications, etc.)

▷ Assist in the planning for, reconstitution of, the national defense forces

▷ Assist in the relocation and rehabilitation of displaced elements of the   population

▷ Supervise and assist in the clearance and removal of unexploded ordnance and mines

Protection of Humanitarian Relief Operations.   Most humanitarian relief is delivered safely and effectively without military assistance. Even in countries where conflict threatens delivery, supply is largely continued by negotiated agreements between local parties and the supervising agency responsible for coordinating relief.   In some UN operations, humanitarian supplies are delivered with the ad hoc assistance of military aircraft and logistic vehicles. The protection of humanitarian relief referred to in this section concerns the organization of a multinational military relief protection force.   The scale of response often dictates the need for a stand-alone operation, as in the case of Northern Iraq (1991).   In every relief protection operation it is expected that the delivery of supplies will be contested locally and that the normal process of lead agency negotiation has proved inadequate, necessitating that a joint multinational task force be organized for delivery.   These activities focus around three primary tasks:

▷ Setting up a mounting base

▷ Providing security for victim population at delivery site

▷ Secure tactical delivery.

Guarantee and Denial of Movements. International operations may be authorized by the Security Council to guarantee or deny movement by ships, aircraft and vehicles in particular areas and routes. They may involve the coordinated presence of warships and combat aircraft in the disputed region.   Operations to guarantee rights of passage may be mounted to ensure the freedom of ships to pass through a threatened sea lane, or for aircraft to reach an encircled city or community.   International operations to deny movement usually focus on the denial of air movement to a regime or government. The concern of the UN may be to prevent the harassment of an unprotected population by the use of combat aircraft or to prevent the delivery of weapons or explosive ordnance onto a civil target. In both cases, these operations may involve highly sophisticated and capable warships and combat aircraft. The safe operation will require the coordinated offensive use of electronic emissions, as well as regular high level intelligence assessments. Their day-to-day deployment will need to be decided by an internationally comprised joint force HQ. It is likely that substantial elements of the force will be provided from an existing military alliance. Operations in this category are distinguished from Level Three Sanctions by their shorter duration, more defined local focus and, therefore, less need for a region-wide consensus.

Level Three Operations

Sanctions. Sanctions, as referred to in the UN charter, usually concern denial of supplies, diplomatic and trading privileges and freedom of movement to an identified aggressor. They are usually only applied when diplomacy and less confrontational methods of conflict resolution have failed. Used on their own without other restraining or coercive measures, sanctions do not usually cause an aggressor to reserve or withdraw from an illegal or war-like activity. However, if applied successfully, sanctions can reduce the war-fighting capability of an aggressor. To achieve a significant level of effectiveness, sanctions must be imposed with the consent of a widely based group of nations including the unanimous support of the regional and neighboring states of the aggressor.

High Intensity Operations. High intensity enforcement operations, as referred to in the UN charter, are the ultimate sanction of the UN Security Council to counter a serious threat to international security. They are only used when all other means of conflict resolution have been exhausted. They may involve a major operation of war against an identified aggressor state. The most powerful combat aircraft, warships and fire support capabilities in service may be deployed, but only the minimum offensive action consistent with achieving the enforcement objective may be used.

OBSTACLES TO REFORM

In the climate of post-Cold War instability, Level Two operations will continue to be the most dynamic in scope and an increasingly important commitment for defence planners. However they lie in a wholly uncharted dimension of military activity; at present, it is not possible to do more than distinguish them conceptually from Level One and Level Three.

The importance of having an effective military presence in Level Two contingencies in two-fold. Firstly, it cannot be acceptable to the international community, in particular to the Security Council, to have their collective writ thwarted locally by small, unrepresentative schisms acting selfishly or even for venal reasons, particularly when this threatens a widely agreed peace process. Secondly, UN contingent-providing nations will not allow their troops, aircraft and warships to be vulnerably exposed in ad hoc military actions, tenuously coordinated on the assumption of a best case scenario, when that assumption is no longer valid.

Establishing an effective military presence does not mean lowering the threshold for the use of force; it is not a proposal to fight for peace. The benefits of an effective military presence lie in operational flexibility. A traditional peacekeeping force invariably has the characteristics of a military garrison, operating from static administrative bases from which it can only deploy in small numbers, for a short duration, in a limit and relatively unsupported operational role. The weakness of this modus operandi is that when the mandate of such a force is unlawfully opposed, even at a very local level (for example a boy beside the track halts the column with his AK-47), it is left with few options except to become dangerously confrontational, or back off. As the elements move further away from their administrative base, their options are reduced. To overcome this inflexibility, a more effective military force must be capable of:

◁   Operating in small patrols for several days out of base at platoon and company strength

◁   Providing requisite transport, logistics, communications

and medical cover for these extended out of base operations
◁ Concentrating swiftly in locally superior strength
◁ Hardening the base areas to sustain random sniping attacks
◁ Coordinating out of base operations with the activities of other UN agencies, NGOs and foreign national assets also present
◁ Calling on high level political support in a local confrontational situation

With these capabilities, an isolated UN patrol faced by the boy beside the track can now:
◁ Be quickly reinforced if necessary
◁ Be logistically sustained in situ for as long as necessary
◁ Bring in political or military representatives of the obstructing party's own affiliation to talk down the impasse
◁ Escort electoral and aid agencies to unlawfully cut off or threatened communities

All the above capabilities, far from relying on the use of armed force, make it a less likely option by giving the isolated patrol commander greater flexibility of response. They also ensure a much more rigorously policed peace agreement which has a chance of standing up to local evasion and sabotage.

However, to make any significant headway in achieving such a capability will first require the UN Secretariat and the leading contributor nations to improve or radically alter: planning and preparation procedures, contingent selection criteria, command and HQ staff selection criteria and logistic flexibility. One of the chief obstacles to this desirable revolution in their operating standards is the absence of a concept development capability in the UN Secretariat. Few senior officials, whose formative experience is derived from the contingencies of peacekeeping in the Cold War era have sufficient knowledge of military practicalities which would enable them to see the dangers of the impending situation. This is aggravated by a caucus within the UN which maintains that the institution already has these capabilities and that the experiences of the Congo, Lebanon and Cyprus equip them to take on Level Two operations or disregard them as a special requirement. Beyond the Secretariat, there is the institutional unwillingness of members to pay for sufficient effective military forces to take part in anything more than a best case scenario.

In conclusion, we are left with the disturbing prospect that in view of the intractable official attitude towards improving the effective standard of military operations and the increasingly harmful consequences of ad hoc planning, we are more likely to witness a major debacle, costing UN lives and damaging UN credibility, than a determined effort to improve operating standards. If this happens, it may through sustained public outcry, fortuitously achieve the much needed revolution in the UN's military efficiency; but, conversely, it may start a public reaction against the UN, in favor of unilateral military action,* and set back the development of a UN response to the contagion of intrastate conflict for many years.

Command and Control Issues for the Military Planner

THE FOLLOWING IS A DISCUSSION of the two papers presented in Session I:

QUESTION: Mr. Connaughton, very early on in your presentation, you used the word "intelligence", I believe the UN was very nervous about the word "intelligence" because it implied, traditional peacekeeping would be seen as less neutral by being in the intelligence acquisition game and thereby servicing war plans. As a legacy of the past, do we need to bury it and face the need for "intelligence" to meet the needs of future operations?

RICHARD CONNAUGHTON: What we have to achieve within the coalition is perhaps a healthier sharing between states of their intelligence. In the past, one used to concentrate on learning about one's enemies, whereas now I think we're going to have to be canny in working out who our future coalition partners are going to be. Therefore, you want a fair amount of intelligence on your friends as well as your enemies. If you go back in time to look at someone like E.H. Carr, who wrote The 20 Years Crisis, he said the problem of collective security requirements is that people say you need them but they never tell you how and why it is to be achieved. I think, today, we can say we understand how and why it can be achieved. One of the problems within the United Nations is that we've had an awful big fund of intelligence, communication, and logistic capabilities under the umbrella of the Security Council's Perm Five, but, in the past, it had been unacceptable to use. Now, we should have a much more conclusive environment within the United Nations for sharing intelligence.

QUESTION: Richard Connaughton talked about command and control and John Mackinlay raised issues of the conceptual approach to what has been so far called peacekeeping operations. I wholeheartedly agree with many of their remarks, though I see there are several difficulties. I should like to present the political side of the coin. The first issue is the question of command and control. I think that it is far easier to organize on a regional basis than it would be on a UN system. I see enormous difficulties for the United Nations to accept the kind of arrangements which Richard Connaughton has suggested, which suggestion is based on the experiences of the Korean Campaign as well as Desert Shield and then Desert Storm. I wonder if either experience is applicable to the UN? Secondly, on John Macinlay's statement on the changing role for the UN, what he is doing is introducing a new concept of operations in the UN. Who is going to manage these operations? The Security Council is not able to handle it. The Security Council has to be altered. What needs to be done with the Security Council to improve its management of these operations? They have not proved to be very agile in managing what is called traditional peacekeeping. They rely entirely on the UN Secretary-General, who together with his staff, are very heavily occupied. At the military advisor level, who is going to manage this? Who is going to make input in management of operations, both at the Security Council and Secretariat levels? How is the Secretary-General going to run this office? My own submission is that it is worth serious questioning that the UN, which is primarily a political body, will be able to adjust itself to be able to manage the middle level of operations. I would submit, strongly, that we consider the choice of regional arrangements which I believe should be preferable and should be the first to which we should turn. Finally, I think it is extremely questionable whether we could change troops trained for regular peacekeeping in the middle of an operation to assume secondary tasks.

JOHN MACKINLAY: I agree with you. The United Nations as an institution is not yet capable of managing a Level-Three operation. I also agree with you that the Security Council which is a political body is quite unsuitable to direct military operation. You have to have a consensus and you need then to translate that consensus into a plan which staff officers can make some sense of on the ground. That machinery is not there. I think I would build on your own point that it is in the mid-level of operations where the UN is, after all, already swimming in this water-with what success I think it is a bit early to say. I think it is in this area we need to build up capability. I think President Bush's recent remarks to the General Assembly were very positive and I hope those remarks survive the U.S. election process. I think there is some evidence in the Pentagon and in the National Security Council that there is a plan to go forward from there. The answer to your question is this—how you are going to do it—you build from what you've got, you improve what you've got, you make your military element, which is already in the United Nations, far more effective by introducing staff officers from capable military armies who have necessary experience. Build up that element inside the UN so that you have in effect a little replica of the NATO headquarters. Then you can turn to them and translate political decisions into something which amounts to a military plan, which is not something that can be done at the moment.

RICHARD CONNAUGHTON: You raise the subject of regional systems and getting them involved. I think in principal we've got to go along with the regional systems and the bigger powers have got to have some bilateral/mulitlateral agreements whereby we can bring into those regions—very much as the U.S. unified command does—the political and military power which that region lacks. Increasingly, we've got to look at presentation. What you have to studiously avoid is the impression that we are exporting the North "Brezhnev Doctrine" to the South. And I think that is a very important point which we need to focus on. You talk about management of operations, there is machinery out there—the Military Staff Committee. The fact is the MSC is in the Charter of the United Nations. The membership of the MSC is anachronistic, but the Charter does provide for the co-opting of interested parties on the Committee. There is no earthly reason why the MSC should not be tasked to provide the Secretary-General the essential information he needs to make meaningful decisions. The Security Council is going to work;

it's a fudge, but I think that once the will is there within the UN
to make it work, what you've got to do is the same that we in the
British Army have got to do in looking at the nature of future
conflict and that is forget what we've got, forget what equipment
we've got, forget what manpower we've got and start with a
fresh piece of paper and start designing what we need for the
future.

QUESTION: My question is on the Military Staff Committee.
The instrument is there and it would appear that this would be a
useful vehicle to do the mundane things that soldiers need to
have done for them before they are committed operationally.
Coming up with common symbology for maps, references,
certain basic logistic contingency requirements, all of these
mundane things of soldiering that tend to be overlooked when a
crisis arises and politicians create a military force, ad hoc. You
have obviously thought a great deal about the Military Staff
Committee, but you seem to assume it is an anachronism.

RICHARD CONNAUGHTON: I think you are right, but it
comes back to the will of states. If we have a change of will of
the major states, then I think we could probably pick up the ball
and run with it. We are aware that the British and the French
and the Pentagon have a view that they don't wish to embrace
the possibilities that are afforded by the Military Staff
Committee. The major hang-up is the question of command.
Operations, I think, divide the three functions: the preparation,
the action, and the aftermath. What we need to do is use the
MSC at the beginning, in terms of preparation and contingency
planning. But I do believe the positions which were taken
perhaps six months ago, may well now today have to be
reviewed and revised to see if we cannot use the Military Staff
Committee effectively to help us deal with looming problems
ahead.

QUESTION: John do you feel the same way about the
potentials of the military Staff Committee?

JOHN MACKINLAY: No. I really failed to encounter a
convincing statement of support from the five embassies who

would be most instrumental in resuscitating the MSC. I think its grown to be a bit like the Beefeaters in the Tower of London who are an extremely attractive tourist item, but their real function, militarily speaking, has disappeared. It will now be extremely difficult to resuscitate the MSC, almost as difficult as to resuscitate the Beefeaters in the Tower of London, And I think rather than trying to, let's go for something which is alive and build on something which is functioning.

QUESTION: First, I want to draw attention to naval cooperation in the UN context. I think that's a vastly overlooked subject.   Second, yesterday the Security Council authorized nations to establish a naval blockade in the Adriatic. The CSCE is a UN-recognized regional organization, and it could have called upon the EC, NATO, or the WEU to direct the operations since the Helsinki Summit identified these three organizations as ones that could be called upon for peacekeeping.   Third, the UN could direct forces for peacekeeping operations. I personally believe the NATO naval on-call mediterranean force could become the naval on-call force for UN.   This could be accomplished without getting to the standing force idea.   I wonder if John Mackinlay had given any thought to this in developing spectrum of different missions that the UN military undertake.

JOHN MACKINLAY: On naval operations, first of all, this is an expanding area and you'd be pleased to know that in Providence, Rhode Island, not very far, after all from Newport, we are actually collaborating very closely with the Naval War College on these things. It is a very interesting area which is going to become much bigger than it is at present.   As to delegation options, we have examples of this already. It is not an option the UN readily will embrace. As we saw in the resolution that was handed to the United States for Desert Storm, it is still an extremely unpopular political option, especially in the General Assembly. Now, I think it is something that we will see happening in Level-Three and the back end of Level-Two operations where the United Nations simply hasn't the needed military personnel. It simply writes a blank check and hands responsibility to another organization—hopefully not the CSCE, because I don't think you'll get much of a change from them. The point about on-call forces, I agree with what you are saying, but there is one point that is worth considering. When a country sends its contingent, that is a highly political affirmation of that operation. If the British send a contingent to Bosnia, that is a very strong signal of support. If you remove that option from countries who are members by saying you've all got to pay us subscriptions anyway and there's none of this business about I'm going to support A but not B, I think that will create a lot of political anxiety among leaders who may very well wish to support an operation in Bosnia but not one in South America. That is always going to be the problem with on-call forces and standing forces where you just snap your fingers at a country and anticipate they will make forces available without any argument.

QUESTION: I think we should clarify thought about the fundamentals of the UN Charter and the terminology we use. We need to recognize the fact that in Korea and in the Desert Storm operations the UN did not authorize anything; the source of authority for the actions that were taken was Article 51, which is also in Chapter 7.   Those were operations of collective self-defense blessed by the Security Council and the blessing was not at all necessary. I think we should be very careful not to mix up actual enforcement actions undertaken by the Security Council and directed by them—which is the conception underlying the Charter—and actions of self-defense most of which never have any UN blessing but which are perfectly legitimate. I also agree with those speakers that have said that the Security Council and the Secretariat are quite incapable of managing military operations beyond the peacekeeping level.   We should concentrate our thinking and forward planning on the institutions which have worked and can work rather than deceiving ourselves and our publics in trying to whip up an enormous tidal wave of approbation, which is a charade.

RICHARD CONNAUGHTON: It is an environment of shifting sand and you must deal with choices that are appropriate to that moment. It was appropriate in Desert Storm to give the United States a blank check and let them direct the operation. I don't think you are going to get a blank check again. It is better to appreciate that world opinion may well not again allow the United States to run a military operation such as Desert Storm.

QUESTION: But remember the United States and other major powers can make the decision that their security is threatened by developments say in Yugoslavia and no approval is required by the Security Council.

RICHARD CONNAUGHTON: I think the problem with Article 51 is that it's been so blatantly abused in the past; but under the Charter, having taken Article 51 action, the states themselves are obliged to report back to Secretary-General as to what action they have taken.

RESPONSE: That's purely informative. The Security Council can't stop an operation of self-defense except by proclaiming that it's become a breach of the peace, violation of the peace and that takes a veto.

QUESTION: I would like to raise a question with regard to command and control and the need for a clear statement of objectives in terms of future United Nations operations. I've been very much attracted to some of the suggestions by the speakers, but let's take a hard case, Somalia. In terms of UN intervention how would you establish a clear mandate of objectives when the majority of UN members are only interested in a humanitarian or relief operation at a time when it is clear that there is anarchy? There is no government in control, and a peace enforcement action is needed to control the environment. How do you get the political side of the house and the military side of the house agreeing on overall objectives and a reasonable plan for implementation?

RICHARD CONNAUGHTON: I think we should not assume that states will automatically intervene in world affairs, because you see in the past, we've looked at intervention in terms of justification and that really, I think, is the reason why so many interventions have failed. Justification by itself does not go far enough. Interventions have to be launched from a rationale which comes from the brain rather than from the heart.

JOHN MACKINLAY: I can understand the problem of Somalia, but the question is, where can the UN successfully operate? Was it possible to successfully operate militarily within Somalia where we have seen a reversion to warlordism? Would we have to go in there and fight the whole array of tribes and warlords? I think really if you do analysis, you may well come to the conclusion that you could not achieve anything militarily in Somalia and, therefore, what you've got to do is look at alternative sets of coercive measures. I personally believe that if no one can make a case for setting up a UN protectorate, then Somalia was the case. But it does seem to me that the world can only really digest perhaps one major crisis at any one time and I'm afraid that Somalia coincided with a lot of what's going wrong in the world. Somalia, I suppose, doesn't have any oil, it's got some rather horrifying pictures but where does the clout come? I think Europe has really awakened to the importance of Yugoslavia and, by Jove, I think we are now beginning to look at Yugoslavia and the Yugoslavian problem with some renewed interest and vigor. I would, however, say that I think Boutros-Ghali's comments pointing fingers at the West saying "You're looking at Yugoslavia, you're not really looking at Somalia," was I think unfair, because certainly Western Europe had brought down a curtain of indifference about what was going on in Yugoslavia until, I think, the penny dropped. Here, we might have a real domino effect sucking into the implosion, states like Greece and Turkey. So I suppose that's a round about way of saying that I think, on occasion, you've got to accept that intervention is not going to work.

JOHN MACKINLAY: I understand that another element of your question is really how do you interest nations in security issues, when their real interest is in the humanitarian side. I had to preach this message in the rather stony fields of Thatcher's Britain. Trying to interest people in the Ministry of Defence in sending British soldiers to countries which have absolutely no foreign policy interest is a pretty difficult thing to do. And it's equally difficult to do in this country. I don't know how a politician is going to persuade "Joe Six-Pack" who apparently runs a garage somewhere in Arkansas, how he is going to want to be involved in a country like Cambodia. I presented this question to an Austrian ambassador, a country which is totally dedicated to this sort of activity, and he had a very good explanation for it, but it wasn't the sort of elevator word-bite that you could use in discussion here today.

The answer to your question, I think, is two-fold. One is that the education process has to start in defense staffs. It is, first of all, a political problem. You can't do much about that, but I think the media, actually is highly instrumental in triggering off a country's response to a situation like the Kurds perched up on their hills in the Turkish border. And then the defense staff and this is happening already.

The fact is that there is no other way to intervene in these places except under the aegis of the UN. In reality, your country and my country really are not lawfully mandated to do this any longer, and the sooner people in the defense planning area understand that and start thinking very seriously about the fact that they have to assign defense planning to participation in these very messy international operations. The third point is that you are talking about security and not humanitarian relief. You are going to have to become involved in this process with a different set of nations because the people who have the capability to respond really very well, like the Nordic nations, to the humanitarian element of these problems are not always the same people who can provide you with the military infrastructure to meet security requirements.

QUESTION: You said you were sowing these seeds on very rocky ground during the Thatcher Administration at the time the British army was also under great pressure to reduce the budget. Did any in the army staff see peacekeeping as an opportunity to maintain a relevance in the budgetary battles that every nation faces?

JOHN MACKINLAY: No. Because, the reduction had just

occurred in the British army and was driven by a need to reduce defense spending, whereas most people who write about these things prefer to reduce an army commensurately with declining interests in foreign policy issues. Obviously, you have a list of tasks and you have a list of troops who have to carry them out, and you can't adjust the right hand column without adjusting the left-hand column. That really has not been done. And so the argument never even got there. And you if you went into the Ministry of Defence, Britain was the one country in the whole of the NATO alliance where, until about three months ago, you could go and ask for the UN desk or spend a long time burrowing through the Ministry of Defence directory and never find it because there wasn't one. The argument never reached the sophistication of your question. It just wasn't a question.

QUESTION: Mr. Connaughton talked about the skills a commander would have to have in the field to implement operations, and in taking that with Mr. Mackinlay's second level activities, which strike me more as policing functions rather than traditional military operations, a major question arises: How do military officers coming out of conventional training have skills to manage these kinds of operations? Neither of the speakers has said anything explicitly, but it seems that, implicitly, the role of command is to separate the belligerents and remain passive in the face of the dynamics of the conflict. Is this an appropriate role for traditional military commanders or are they, in fact, on a continuous basis conflict mediators for the belligerents at a local level? And if so, where do they get the training to do this. Is this the responsibility of the sponsoring country? Is this a function of the United Nations?   Where do these military commanders get the skills to deal with an essentially non-traditional military situation?

JOHN MACKINLAY: Is this a military role? Yes, coming from the army that I come from, it certainly is. But in the U.S., it probably isn't quite so clear cut because yours is an army where the infantry do the infantry things and the cavalry do the cavalry things and they don't have to go to Northern Ireland once every three years where they have to clear their mind about some of these ideas and have to function on the ground. I think that in the case of the U.S., you have a problem.

Nevertheless, it is a military role, and I would advise people in the Pentagon who are interested in preserving the size of both the infantry and the cavalry to become a little more flexible, because its a very useful second string to have on your bow. Another reason why it is a military role is because who else are you going to send to that God-forsaken "pitch up" against the Thai border in Cambodia to patrol with your blue flag along those tracks, which could very easily be mined. And if you're going to tell me it's the police, I want you to nominate for me a police force that we all know that is capable of sending constables that could survive under those conditions and behave in the correct way. I don't know of a police force in my country that could possibly deploy policemen into that situation.

How to train them? Well you could train a military officer to do almost anything. The fact is you've got to start off by wanting him to train. I think that if President Bush's suggestion to the General Assembly about converting Ft. Dix into an area where these things could be done practically, that is the sort of direction we should be taking. Why haven't we got a United Nations staff college? We've got a staff college for practically every alliance and former military activity there is, but it seems so obvious that we should have one to train staff officers. When the officer has that qualification you know the man is fit to take part on a UN staff. We should have schools which go into the Level-Two and Level-Three areas because both are really much more difficult.

RICHARD CONNAUGHTON: In terms of using military force in the manner in which you are suggesting, either it is intuitive or you have to train for it. I think you have also to address the aftermath. And one thing that the military services can assist with is the humanitarian side of operations. I think for governmental organizations this is relatively easy. There is no reason why today we shouldn't be looking at government organizations to give them the infrastructure and military support they need. The problem area is going to be Non-Governmental Organizations (NGOs), you know, the well intentioned people who took a lot of medical support and, actually, in terms of raising follow-on funds, have to seem to be untarnished. I would agree with John that the British have a tradition of being involved in this area. And it is an area which any other state could actually start to begin working on.

Critical Considerations for
the Military Commander

THE FOLLOWING DISCUSSION FEATURED the insights and comments of military officers with personal experience in carrying out UN peacekeeping operations:

JOHN SEWALL: The focus in this session will be on implications for military planners who are asked to undertake a peacekeeping mission for the UN—whether it is an individual observer operation, in the traditional ideal world of peacekeeping, or one involving small size units or even larger size units in what has been described this morning as Level-Two or Level-Three operations. Permit me to introduce the members of the panel. Brigadier General Ian Douglas is currently the Canadian Military Attache here in Washington. BG Douglas has had experience at the practitioner field level when he was involved in a peacekeeping operational tour in Cyprus. He has commanded three mechanized commandos of the fourth Canadian mechanized brigade group in Germany. He has also commanded the Canadian airborne regiment in "Petawawar." BG Douglas was Chief of Staff of the UN Peacekeeping Mission in Central America from December '89 until December '90, and has served as peacekeeping advisor in military headquarters in Ottawa.

Alos on the panel is Colonel Bruce Osborn, who is with the Australian Mission to the United Nations in New York. In terms of UN experience, Bruce was posted as the land staff officer in the Directorate of Joint Operations of Headquarters of the Australian Defence Force and was, in that capacity, responsible for management of Australian participation in both policy and operational aspects of UN peacekeeping operations. He has most recently (January '91) been posted to New York as the military advisor to the Australian Mission to the United Nations.

Lieutenant Colonel Bill Spracher is a Foreign Area Officer or "FAO," which is a specialty in the United States Army that concentrates on training and schooling in regional specialties. You will find that a good percentage of US observers in peacekeeping have been, in fact, FAO officers. He is a military intelligence officer who has also been an instructor at West Point. Bill spent a lot of time in Panama. As a Latin America specialist, you might wonder why he ended up in the Western Sahara. That may indicate something about US planning, which we hope to correct. At any rate, he was military assistant to the force commander, United Nations Mission for the Referendum in Western Sahara, MINURSO.

Major George Steuber is currently a student at Ft. Leavenworth, at the US Army Command and General Staff College. He also is a Foreign Area Officer whose specialty is SE Asia. He went to the Royal Thai Army Command and Staff College and spent a considerable amount of his career in the Pacific region. Most recently, he was in SE Asia with the United Nations advanced mission in Cambodia and the UN Transitional Authority in Cambodia (UNTAC). He was an operations officer for Team Delta, the military liaison detachment established at the Khmer People's National Liberation Armed Forces Headquarters, and then he moved to Phnom Penh. Lastly, he became Lt Gen John Sanderson's personal representative in Kamponton Province.

With these brief introductions let me turn to our first panel expert, General Douglas.

GENERAL I.C. DOUGLAS: None of what I heard this morning from the academic side of the house disagreed in any way, shape or form, seriously, with what I had experienced. Therefore, I would hope to offer you some practical observations which we can apply to the rather more academic solutions that were put forward this morning. I will try to be frank without being rude because some of the problems we encountered in setting up the new mission in Central America were caused by individuals in the United Nations in New York. New York has many good people; they also have some not so good people, which is the same with any bureaucracy. But what you don't have in UN missions is the military hierarchy needed to make the decisions for you when it affects the soldier in the field. You have got to go along with what is fundamentally a civilian hierarchy. This sometimes flies in the face of the military requirement.

I will go over very quickly and generally the chronology of what I saw as we deployed down into Central America, how our mandate changed and we went from being a level-one mission to a level-two mission without any appreciation of the differences by Headquarters New York. That should become clear as we talk about some of the problems we faced as we went from a simple observer mission to one that had to interpose itself between the Contras and the Sandinistas, who didn't talk to each other—indeed who were still shooting each other in some places—and try to bring some sense to the whole situation and eventually to demobilize the Contra army. The reconnaissance for ANOOKA was carried out by an ad hoc team, and if there is one word to describe UN operations as far as I saw it was "ad hocery". The military staff was not capable, based on their numbers. They were overwhelmed by the jobs in front of them. Initially, you had reconnaissance teams made up of members from different countries who went down to study the situation. They came back and formulated the plan which was rubber stamped by headquarters staff. The staff themselves were not capable of formulating what I would call a proper military estimate. The mandate which we were given was "mission impossible". It was to patrol and prevent the crossing of frontiers of the signatory states for military purposes by either side, including the movement of weapons and military equipment across the borders. Any one who has looked at the borders of those two countries will know that is impossible unless you have an army of some 50,000 to 100,000 men. The idea of putting a mission in there, I think, was a calculated risk and absolutely right. In other words, you had the five Central American countries who had agreed to the efforts, and the UN decided to put the mission in there regardless of how impossible it was with a view ultimately of demobilizing the Contras, which indeed worked out.

We went down there and started setting up the organization as best we could, setting up headquarters, setting up observation posts along the border, setting up our network with the Contras, who indeed controlled a good part of the border, and with the Sandinistas. We never did, in my tour of duty, come to grips with the problem on the Salvadorean border which has subsequently been resolved by other missions. When we became aware of the fact that the demobilization of the Contras was to take place, we were told that we, the observer mission, would have to do it, and if we really needed it, the UN was prepared to give us a platoon of military policemen to accomplish it. This was a civilian estimate. We did a very rough military estimate and decided it would take at least one and probably two reinforced battalions to do what was required. It needed a logistics organization which didn't exist in the observer mission, and it needed fantastic amounts of helicopter support.

The UN's response when we said we needed logistics was, "Well you observers are getting $65 a day, why don't you just buy what you need?" This was a complete misconception of how you have to support something which has gone from an observer mission to putting battalions and companies of soldiers into the field. Headquarters in New York never did comprehend that. What we had to do was completely ad hoc the logistics organization, which was to steal observers who were of a logistics persuasion, get a contracting officer out of the UN, and set up our own organization. My fleet of trucks was a fleet of banana trucks, which I leased from the Great Pacific Banana Company in Honduras. The helicopters, we rented. Everything was ad hoc, and we made it with the skin of our teeth. In one particular site in the Nicaraguan jungle, every observer came down with a parasite that was potentially fatal; it would take at least a year for them to be cured and, indeed, some of them are still suffering from it today. We're just lucky we didn't lose some men to the parasite. All of this is to say the structure to support the military in the United Nations, be it from an operational military point of view or from a logistics view, is not there. That problem has to be resolved.

The solution, as I would see it, lies in the restructuring, remandating of the military advisory staff to the Secretary-General. The analogy I make is to an organization called AMFL, the Allied Command Europe Mobile Force, which has existed for 40 years in NATO. The idea of the large standing UN force has been discussed ad nauseum and has been rejected over the years.

I don't think you can have a large division or indeed corps-sized force that stood ready for UN operations, but what you do need is a properly constituted, experienced and mandated miliary staff that can do a number of things. It can do the planning, it can look after the staff lists, it can look after the skeletal SOPs, it can look after the training of the units which are earmarked in different countries for UN operations. It might be a brigade sized force with fifteen countries volunteering to contribute to it. Perhaps some would not be suitable to a particular country; maybe that particular country would not wish to go into a particular operation. You establish sufficient flexibility in the numbers of units you have established to meet such a contingency so that you do not have to ad hoc everything from the bottom up. I think that an organization of some 26 to 30 military people could organize that. Now perhaps they wouldn't deploy as AMFL brigade headquarters, but they would be able to do the planning and to brief the brigade and/or division headquarters getting ready to go into any area of the world. I think that such an arrangement is essential if you are going to improve whatever we are going to get out of the Secretary-General's staff, which at the moment is ad hocery for every mission.

There are training requirements that we have for UN forces. The best qualified UN type organization is a general purpose military unit. You can take a well-trained unit that's ready to go into operations in NATO, if you will, and you can turn them into a peacekeeping force very quickly. You cannot do it the other way around. You can't develop a peacekeeping force and then turn it into a general purpose force without extensive retraining and re-equipping. That is one of the tenets on which we have established our UN contribution over the years. We send trained combat-ready forces. Notwithstanding that, you will need some training, but not very much. You have to train in your staff colleges to make sure your officer corps is ready to take off that warrior's perspective or viewpoint in life, and put on that of the peacekeeper, of the mediator or whatever the situation calls for. We figure we can do that in our staff college with a weeks' course; before observer missions, we have a two-week program which we feel is sufficient to bring the individual up to standard on such things as sensitivities of the area, area studies, that sort of thing. Beyond that, of course, you have language studies, but the training requirement as opposed to what has been suggested by others that we have peacekeeping academies, peacekeeping universities, is not seen as needed in the Canadian army. The bottom line is that the units have to be ready to go to Level-Two and Level-Three operations which involves your general purpose training and equipped organizations.

COLONEL BRUCE OSBORN: I thought it might be useful to look at this from the New York Headquarters perspective. I suspect, as is always the case, a number of perspectives on this peacekeeping business exist and I think it totally proper to consider this subject from all angles. One thing is clear—all our perceptions of peacekeeping have changed dramatically. Firstly, it is abundantly clear to me that, since 1988, the world around us has changed dramatically in every shape and form.   Who would have predicted where we would be today four years ago. Yet, in many respects, the United Nations really has not changed. This is no direct criticism of those who lead the UN, but is a reflection of the fact that the UN is a bureaucracy. To change the system is going to take some time. I also do not wish to dampen anybody's enthusiasm, but my own view is that it's going to change incredibly slowly. The one thing that impressed me after I got to New York was to find out how political the United Nations was. It is wrong for any nation to think it can go to New York because of who they are and change the system overnight. There are 179 member states, soon to become 180, who all go to the United Nations it seems to me, to look after their own vested interests. They very much have an interest in the world and they'll pursue those interests, but to a large extent they are pursuing them for their own benefit. Now that in itself is not wrong. I see my country pursuing the same course, but the reality is that you are working in a political organization where decisions are made through committees, that is by consensus. Now you don't have to be terribly intelligent to realize that the system is very slow. Decisions normally end up being watered down to something which is diluted.

The United Nations, since the end of the Cold War, I would have thought would have been terribly open and transparent.

Instead, you would believe that the Cold War is at its height at the present time in the United Nations. The things which we would expect to be readily available to us in terms of information is not available—just the opposite is the case. It strikes me that the principal problem is that many of those who were part and parcel of the old United Nations are still there, and they haven't been able to adapt to the realities of the new world. You notice I didn't say "New World Order".

If I might quickly address the Agenda for Peace—and I'm sure some of my colleagues might have different views—I represent my country in the Special Committee on Peacekeeping Operations, a committee of 34 nations which really, in a practical way, considers peacekeeping perhaps more than any other organization in the UN. Most recently, as late as yesterday, the Special Committee was considering the item of peacekeeping, and I might offer some impressions as to where the *Agenda for Peace* report is going. In the area of preventive diplomacy, there is broad support for enhanced preventive diplomacy. Indeed, it is the most popular part of the Secretary-General's report. I think it is popular because people see the prospect of finding a solution to a problem, before it becomes a conflict, as the way to go. My own view is there will be progress in that area. But it is going to be slow because for the Secretary-General to have a capability to make independent assessments and decisions on a timely basis requires enormous resources. He is not going to have adequate resources to provide the information, and he, therefore, is going to rely on member states. Nevertheless, he is still going to need some sort of independent assessment capability to make those decisions.

In the area of peacekeeping, there is broad support for enhanced peacekeeping capabilities within the United Nations. There are many subareas in this report, but by and large there is support for funding arrangements to be made more readily available. In the area of preventive deployment, there is lukewarm support. Many countries, and particularly the non-aligned countries and those countries who see themselves as being the object of preventive deployments are concerned about issues of national sovereignty. There is also a question amongst the membership at large relating to the neutrality of the United

Nations in various situations. My own view is—listening to my colleagues in and around New York—that it might work in certain circumstances. For example, if another Saddam Hussein comes along, I think that's a set of circumstances where military action will be acceptable.

But let us discuss another more clouded area, the question of enforcement action under Article 43. Here, the reality is that the majority of the membership, as I see it, is opposed to that sort of activity at the present time. I suggest that it is not going to go anywhere for some considerable period of time. Now, I know that's a very bold statement, but that's the reality of the current political environment. It may change dramatically if circumstances change.

I just wanted to briefly touch upon Headquarters planning. The reality is that planning for peacekeeping operations does not occur in the United Nations. At best, we have developed a concept, and that concept becomes the basis on which things happen. But, in the real sense of planning, it just simply does not occur. I personally, and many of my colleagues, see this lack of proactive planning as being the fundamental problem which the United Nations faces, and in my view, it is costing enormous sums of money and, indeed, putting service personnel's lives at stake. The Security Council, on the 29th of October, recognized something which the Committee of 34 had been calling for over many years, namely, that there needs to be some enhancement of the planning capability. But yet having said that, there remains great resistance to it. At a time when we are talking about expanding the capabilities of the United Nations, it seems to me that in the case of Somalia, and in the case of UNPROFOR (that is Yugoslavia) the members of the United Nations were not willing to provide the needed resources. And I mention that because I think the membership has reached saturation point in terms of what it is prepared to support. I know that, for instance, my country and many others, at a time when our defense forces are downsizing and our defense budgets and overall budgets are being reduced, are asked to do more and more in terms of deploying for peacekeeping. The reality is that many of us cannot afford to do much more, and that's an important point to take on board.

The other point is that it is obvious to many of the

developing countries that the United Nations—sorry, the stronger members of the United Nations—are prepared to deploy peacekeeping forces to countries in their region to deal with problems that affect them directly. I guess the people being discussed see it as a "rich man-poor man" approach. The other reality in terms of resources is simply that none of us have any spare logistics sitting on the shelf, except perhaps for some of the larger countries. I mean the reality is we just do not have spare logistics units in Australia. They are civilianizing us to the greatest extent possible. We just do not have the sort of organization which Somalia calls for. Somehow, the United Nations has got to deal with that problem. And the final point I'll make is that many members of the United Nations are critical of the Security Council, because they see it increasingly making decisions without consultation with the rest of the UN organization. I will simply put it up the flagpole that at a time when we're trying to change things, these other countries are more and more concerned that the Security Council is acting as the sole decisionmaking body of the United Nations.

LIEUTENANT COLONEL BILL SPRACHER: I plan to give you a fairly recent perspective from ground level in a small mission that probably epitomizes all the kinds of problems we are talking about and some others that are unique to it. I will try to steer away from political issues, but in my role as the military assistant to the force commander in the Western Sahara, I could not avoid politics. UN Mission for the Referendum in Western Sahara (MINURSO) is a very small and not very well known mission of the United Nations. It was established in September of 1991, and initially it was a limited observer mission, to be in the field for a few months. The peace process was expected to move along fairly expeditiously. The peace process has not moved along as anticipated and MINURSO remains a limited observer mission. And that goes at the heart of a lot of the problems I wish to address. Initially, it was envisioned that MINURSO would have a military force of 1,695 personnel, 550 of whom would be military observers. As of the time I left at the end of July 1992, we had around 350 military, 230 of whom were military observers. The military component was given the mandate to monitor and verify the cessation of hostilities between Moroccan and Polisario forces, the withdrawal of Moroccan forces and the confinement of Polisario forces as agreed upon by both parties. This was in a peace plan signed in 1988. And, finally, to establish a climate of confidence, security and stability conducive to the holding of a referendum.

Briefly, Morocco, which is one of the parties to the conflict, considers Western Sahara as another of its provinces. Moroccans just refer to it as "Sahara". Morocco effectively occupies the western two-thirds of that territory. The Polisario guerrillas, basically Saharawi indigenous peoples, who had been fighting for the independence of the territory, occupy the eastern one-third of the area. It is almost like a World War I situation; the Moroccans have built a berm, 2,000 kilometers long right down the center of the territory. They occupy it much like a Maginot Line with a little less technology perhaps from the World War I time frame. So, in one way, this is a very primitive type military set-up. Nevertheless, there were a lot of military clashes over the years, most recently immediately before the cease-fire went into effect, i.e., in September of 1991, when the Moroccans conducted air strikes against Polisario in an attempt to establish good positions before the cease-fire. Since the MINURSO military force has been deployed, small though it is, it has been successful in preventing an outbreak of hostilities. There have been no casualties as a result of fire, most of the casualties have been a result of land mines. So even though it is a limited deployment, and even though the mandate is very ambitious, for that portion of the mandate that this limited military force was established to meet, they have been very successful.

Initially, a referendum was to be held as early as January 1992. I got there in the middle of February. I said "Well how did the referendum go?" They said "It didn't," and it still hasn't been conducted—although as I understand since I departed there has been some progress, mainly from the New York end rather than on-site.

There are 26 countries represented in the small MINURSO military force. This force has the distinction of being the first UN military force that has observers from all five permanent members of the Security Council. We also had the distinction of being the first UN mission that was charged to not just monitor elections but actually to organize and implement a referendum. Now that was not our objective as a military force; we were deployed to create a climate of confidence so this could happen. We think we did the job, but, for whatever reasons, we had not progressed as fast as we would have liked. I was the senior US military observer. We had a contingent of 30. Three countries were tied for the largest contingent, the other two being France and China. We had all four Services of the US represented. The Army was the executive agent, and of half of those thirty, 15 were from the Army and five each were from the other three Services. All were individual observers. All were farmed out to one of the ten team sites or one of the three sector headquarters, and a handful worked in the force headquarters. This is not the kind of mission where we had actual infantry battalions on the ground. The only contingents that operated as national contingents were our good friends the Australians, who had an outstanding signals contingent of approximately 45 folks. They've been in the peacekeeping business a long time, and they were invaluable in helping us new guys on the block figure out how to survive in a desert environment.

The Canadians had not only the force commander at the time, but also when I got there all the clerks and movement control personnel. The largest contingent, interestingly, was the Swiss medical unit, which, when I arrived, had about eighty folks building several clinics. Switzerland is not a member of the United Nations, but for those kinds of humanitarian efforts, they participate—and they were first class. The medical support was the best kind of support we had over there.

Problems: I do not want to be pessimistic, so I will give the bad stuff first and end up with the good stuff. I was part of the second contingent of Americans to arrive. This is a new experience for Americans. There were a lot of lessons to be learned on the training, equipping, preparing, pre-briefing and all that sort of thing. The US Army has figured it out now, and I think we've got a good system in place. I do not think some of my fellow observers knew where the Western Sahara was until they got off the plane. They were by and large volunteers, and they learned very quickly. Those things are getting fixed. Not only were the Australians helpful, but also the Canadians, who were there in large numbers—-we borrowed heavily from their little booklets on peacekeeping operations. They had equipment recognition manuals, all these kinds of things. So we plagiarized from them; now we're starting to produce our own. That's the kind of thing that is essential for observers to do their jobs well. MINURSO had no air conditioning in the force headquarters. We were in a modified elementary school and it was pretty miserable. There was no air conditioning anywhere when arrived. I am happy to say I spent a large portion of time there working on living and working conditions. The Canadian company, Weather Haven, brought in shelters and we spent about three months emplacing those. The site folks went out on mobile patrols riding in Nissan four by four vehicles, grading violations on both sides. These were primarily unauthorized overflights, unauthorized movements, and the most serious during the first few months I was there, unauthorized fortifications—berm construction by the Moroccans.

I will echo what has been said before. Logistics was the biggest problem. I was briefed before I went over there that logistics was the Achilles heel of MINURSO; when I departed six months later, it was still the Achilles heel. In the initial plan, there was supposed to be a Polish logistics battalion. We fought for months to get that, and it never arrived. It got to the point where we would have liked to have had a Polish logistics squad, just a couple of truck drivers, but we could not get them,   I know that the UN is stretched thin, and I know there are political considerations, but we had a Canadian two-star general who pulled his hair out trying to convince New York that without effective logistics you cannot do your job. So, what did we have? We had individual observers who were "humping" fuel barrels, who were escorting trailers carrying fuel, who were spending probably as much time doing logistics duties just to support their own team site as they were assuming military operational duties. That cannot continue. We were very innovative. We could do things on our own initiative, but you cannot do that on a permanent basis and still do your operational mission.

I won't get into problems with cooperation by the various parties to the conflict because that's really a political issue. However, that also affects the mentality of observers when they are reporting violations and they are left with the perception that these things are going into a dark hole somewhere and no one at either UN Headquarters or in the Security Council is taking note of these. Now, we were sort of in a vacuum; we did know a great deal about what was going on in New York, and I guess from a purely objective military standpoint that was all to the good. But, I think it would help observers if they knew a little bit more about the policy implications of what they are doing, and if they knew at least something about what their own country's position is regarding a particular conflict. I think they could do their job better. The military force, which was the only game in town—and I think pretty much still is—unfortunately, got blamed by the parties for some of these political failures. When you are out there talking to a Polisario leader or a Moroccan general and you're wearing a blue beret and they perceive that the UN is not objective, they blame you.

Many times my boss had to explain to them, "I have a narrow military mandate. This is what I'm here to do, that's what I'm doing, and just transmit your concerns about the political impasse back to New York".

Finally, we had numerous mine incidents. There are mines in the Western Sahara left over from the days when the territory was a Spanish colony. There were mines emplaced by the Moroccans around this berm; there are mines emplaced by the Polisario, who sneak up and steal the Moroccan mines and replant them without marking where they are located. The problem was that we did not know where they were, and the Moroccans did not share minefield data they had. One of our vehicles ran over an anti-tank mine and, if anybody wants to see what an anti-tank mine does to a Nissan four by four, I've got some pictures up here I can show you. We have an Air Force officer walking around with a purple heart as a result of that incident. We were very lucky, and I'm pleased with that.

Finally, we end up on some good points. I think this mission was sort of the epitome of what can be done in a post-Cold War environment. Here we have former antagonists working together. We were flying in all-Soviet aircraft, purchased on contract; we had helicopters flown by Soviet crews; we had cargo planes flown by Romanian crews, and VIP aircraft flown by

Czechoslovakian crews. I asked why we had all these "Eastern bloc" aircraft, and they said those countries were the lowest bidders and had a lot of aircraft they were trying to get rid of. The aircraft worked very well.

I want talk a little bit about professional development to wrap-up. I think a tour like this, no matter how many frustrations are experienced, is outstanding training for a line military officer. I cannot really say I'm a line military officer. I'm more of a pol-mil person, a Foreign Area Officer, and General Sewall is right some of the Foreign Area Officers who were in the Sahara did very well because they were trained in dealing with national sensitivities, cultural awareness, languages and all that kind of stuff. But we had a large number of folks who were just line officers, and it was hard to find enough personnel who spoke Arabic, French, and Spanish. That's how I got there, by the way, as a Latin America specialist who had worked for a Peruvian general who spoke French and Spanish quite well, but who could not speak not much English, although that was the working language of the mission—so I got some good Latin American training there in the Western Sahara. I also would say with respect to special forces personnel that, they do very well in this kind of assignment because they're used to being deployed in small numbers or individually to foreign areas. They have the necessary skills; they have the little manuals tied down in their pants pockets-you know, little phrase books, all that kind of stuff. Little things that, had we been in the peacekeeping business a long time, we would have figured out. I think the US is now on the road to being very good at this type of activity. From a professional development standpoint, however, I said I was there six months, and the reason this was a six month TDY tour was partially because of the uncertainty regarding the future of this particular mission. I think for continuity purposes it should have been a one year tour, and I told my bosses that I, as a bachelor, would have loved to spend one year in the Sahara. Some of the young officers who were married and were loaned by Ft. Bragg were ready to go back to their regular units after six months.

I asked my personnel assignments officer for an evaluation when I returned. I said what does a UN assignment do to a guy's career; he said, "Well, one time probably wouldn't hurt any, but I wouldn't do it on a repetitive basis." That's the kind of mentality we have to deal with when we attempt to get good folks who have this experience and want to go back for additional UN assignments. Now, I am not saying that we should do like some countries (like Ireland), some of whose military personnel have concentrated their entire careers from one mission to the other. But I think we have to educate our leadership at least here in the United States that this is the future, this is the kind of thing that militaries are going to do in the foreseeable future. It is better to send 30 military personnel out than an entire brigade or an entire division. A final note: the morale of our people in MINURSO, despite the frustrations, was high because we kept stroking them, and asking them "Have any of our folks been killed by mine incidents?" We came close a few times, but the fact that the ceasefire is holding , I think, is reason for patting our people on the back and saying a limited military observer mission can do some very good things.

MAJOR GEORGE STEUBER: Well, having served six months on one of those Level-Two peacekeeping operations with a low level of military competence, I can say that there are some major problems that, if not resolved, are going to have some grave consequences for UN missions in the future. I think the first thing that needs to be addressed when you have a UN mission of the comprehensive scope of Cambodia is that the UN political and military leadership needs to decide what they are going to do to achieve success. It was not done in Cambodia, and, by the sound of it, has not been done in most of the other UN missions. That is absolutely crucial. What do you do when a representative of the Australian army is shot at while flying in a United Nations helicopter (bright white with black United Nations over it and blue UN flags) and you pinpoint who has done it? What happens when the Khmer Rouge keeps stalling a peace settlement that they have signed and nobody is willing to take the political and economic sanctions necessary to stop that? These have to be addressed before you ever put anybody on the ground, and they obviously have not been addressed.

Coordination between United Nations agencies: Our mission

in Cambodia as UNAMIC, United Nations Advanced Mission in Cambodia and United Nations Transitional Authority in Cambodia, UNTAC, was literally to take over the country: to stop four fighting factions from continued fighting and take over the ministry of foreign affairs, the ministry of the interior, the ministry of finance, and everything else and run a country until national elections were held, and Cambodia could become Cambodia again.

To accomplish this, we had to take four fighting factions—100% of them, some 220,000 soldiers—regroup them, canton them, disarm them, and demobilize 70% of them. And to do this, we were given 11 infantry battalions spread throughout the country, in a country that no longer has an infrastructure, does not have telephones, does not have roads, does not have railroads, does not have anything. Rather a large order. And again without consensus on how to achieve this, it is rather difficult to do it.

Planning: There was no planning to speak of for UNTAC. I got to Cambodia on the 8th of December 1991, one month after the initial group had come into country, and I deployed to my field site on the Thai-Cambodian border on the 22nd. In between, we played musical headquarters. We changed headquarters three different times because the civilian component couldn't agree with the military component on where we should put a headquarters—that's after they had already been there for a month.

Logistics: We got there and they said, "Well, you're getting subsistence allowance, why should we support you? Go buy it." Well, that's fine if you've got a place to buy it, but Cambodia's been at war for 20 years and the places to buy things are very limited. The things you can buy are even more limited. That presents a bit of a problem. There really was no planning. We deployed on the 22nd of December to three team sites (we were just observers at the time), five members to an observer team plus three Australian communicators and support. By the way I'd like to put in a plug for the Australians. If the Australians had not been in that mission, UNTAC and UNAMIC would have failed in January at the latest, rather than having plugged along minimally successfully for one year now. The Australians saved our butts, they provided us with security; they sent medics with each one of the teams, so if we had stepped on one of the three to four million mines emplaced out there, somebody would have been able to take care of us, because the UN mission obviously could not.

They deployed us without maps. Now I'm here to tell you that if you go into an area, it would be nice to know where you are. It would be nice to know where you are going to site these camps to canton some 220-odd thousand people. I tried for two months to secure maps and, finally, I had to go back down to Phnom Penh and man-handle the S-3 and literally threaten his life so that I could get money to buy them on the black market. They were not available through UN channels. That's ludicrous to say the least. A little bit of planning would have been nice going in. Logistics did not get any better when I left at the end of six months. The last thing I did before I left was get in a commandeered Toyota four-by-four, load 18 five-gallon water jerrys in the back and drive 240 kilometers to my team site so that I could give them the first water they had had in two weeks. That's not good after six months.

The Staff: The staff was really unique. We had a chief of staff who spoke Polish, and some very broken French, but no English. Needless to say, he was not really in charge of the staff. My team leader was an Argentinean officer whom I admired greatly. He taught himself to speak, read and write English in the six months that he was there, but to start out, he spoke none. One of my Australian's parents were Chilean, and he spoke a little Spanish at home, so we used him to speak to my team leader. Again, it does not make for really good crisp execution of a mission if you cannot speak to your team leader.

Now we overcame those sorts of things, but staff planning is critical. As long as you have a staff that is made up of politically appointed officers, there is no way of establishing responsibility for executing the mission, and that's a critical item as you may well imagine. That need not happen.

I'm here to tell you that General Sanderson, the commander of the UNTAC mission, was absolutely hamstrung by the inability to appoint the people that he needed for critical staff functions. The other thing is this: just because a gentleman walks through the door and has a specific rank on his shoulder and holds a specific position within his military does not mean that he knows a damned thing about a military operation. There are some people out there who are totally incompetent. It is not their fault. They mean well and, for their own operations, they might even do a good job.

We are talking about a 20,000-person operation in Cambodia spread out over an entire country. That is a large undertaking and it demands that the people in key staff positions be competent. One way to get around that is through staff training. I think it is crucial that a school be established that will train UN staff officers. I believe that, because I am currently at the Command and General Staff College—and I believe we turn out a good product—most of the other staff colleges represented by the officers here today turn out good products. We have many hundreds of foreign officers that attend such colleges.

That does not mean that a foreign staff officer is going to be on a UN mission. It does mean that somewhere in his military career, he will be in a functioning position. If you have a UN staff training school, hopefully, the UN will also prepare some doctrine on how it will conduct its field operations. That doctrine needs to be taught at a UN staff college so that when a mission goes into an area, that staff can function effectively.   In Cambodia we have a signals mission. The Australians provided the national contingent. We have engineers; the New Zealanders came in and did that mission. The French provided us with our initial airlift.   Those were national contingents.   Give me a national contingent headquarters; they will at least have common operating doctrine and know how to do things, and I can then put a staff officer from another nation at the head of it.   Two different ways to meet the need, but it is absolutely essential, that those things be done.

Execution: Again, as long as you have political people in senior staff level positions that are not held accountable for what they're doing and cannot be fired by the commander for incompetence, you will have very poor execution. The three types of people I encountered on a UN operation were: those that knew how to do the job and were motivated to do the job; those that would have liked to do the job, but lacked the tools; and those that, quite frankly, did not give a damn and were drawing $110-$145 a day to go back to their country rich. Now that's a terrible indictment, but, that's what's going on out there. That needs to stop. If the United Nations becomes a competent military organization, you can stop that. If you provide that military force with good logistics, and a good workable plan, I won't need to pay an observer $145 a day. And quite frankly, that's not necessary anyway, because in Cambodia at $145 a day I could own large portions of Cambodia. You know it only takes about $15.00 a day maximum if you want to live like a king in Cambodia, unless you're living in Phnom Penh—which, by the way, is where the UN headquarters happens to be, and that's why it is at $145 a day.

These things are not necessary. If I have a good functioning military organization, I can take care of my people without paying those kinds of dollars. And those kinds of dollars distort the economy. We do more harm in Cambodia and other small countries by paying these people these exorbitant sums. Take Kompong Thom province. You have an Indonesian battalion there now; they aren't being paid $145 a day, but their normal pay plus the increment that they get from the United Nations would make them millionaires in Cambodia. As a result, you cannot buy chickens on the market anymore and you cannot buy rice. So what do the Cambodians get? They get the cracked broken rice that nobody else will buy; they get the scrawny chickens they raise or that nobody else will take. You create another problem by just deploying a United Nations force. The IMF was looking at this problem. Unfortunately, because of a lack of coordination between agencies, nothing ever got done about this. These are some really key problems that go with a United Nations mission. That's why it is imperative that planning go on before you ever commit anybody to this type of operation.

Training: The United States has a pretty good training program for Foreign Area Officers. When I went to the Thai Command and General Staff College on the Thai border, most of the people in the military commands along the border were classmates of mine, at least at the junior and mid-officer level. It helped greatly with coordination. I worked with the Khmer Peoples National Liberation Armed Forces initially. They are located on the Thai border, and all speak Thai. Not a problem.

I didn't need an interpreter. There aren't any interpreters in Cambodia anymore. Pol Pot destroyed the educational system.

The only people you'll find there that are bilingual are those of the older generation. They speak French, and some that had associated with Americans speak English; but the whole middle level of population—all your junior leaders—speak neither French nor English. So somebody, if you're going in as an observer team, had better have access to good interpreters or be able to speak the language. That's really key in training.

As far as major units, I absolutely agree, a well-trained infantry or armor or mechanized infantry unit can go in and do any mission you want them to do. And they can do so easily with a minimum amount of training. They need to know the historical background of the conflict so they do not do stupid things, as well as the motives of the factions that are in the conflict. They need to know a little bit about the local culture, so they do not do culturally unacceptable things.

For example, at Battambang, a freak wind came up. The United Nations team suddenly heard small arms fire breaking out at the far end of town. Battambang is not a very secure area and, as this small arms fire increased in intensity and started rolling towards the team location, they believed they were under major ground attack. They started to get on the radio, were ready to call for an extraction, when some of the folks on the roof of the hotel where they were located looked outside and saw in fact that the Cambodians were just firing up in the air to "stop the wind". That's a normal Cambodian practice. When it is windy, when a storm approaches, they shoot in the air and the wind stops, hopefully.

Such a practice can cause problems. If you have untrained UN people in a situation like that, they may respond with firing of their own. So the cultural sensitivities need to be part of training for mission participants. You need to have your people understand that they are going into an austere environment. One of the things that UNTAC did was they deployed some police along the border between Cambodia and Vietnam. And after two weeks of one policeman crying his eyes out every single day, they decided that maybe that was a bad idea and repatriated him. You take any police officer out of a major metropolitan area and tell him he's got to do these sorts of things in the wilds of

Cambodia, or the wilds of Somalia, it poses major problems. An Australian constable from the "out back" would probably be able to do that sort of thing—and, in fact, they do that sort of training in other areas—but you have to think about who you are trying to put in what situation and then again this goes back to planning. What forces are applicable and where should they be going? What should their jobs be? I think that President Bush's speech to the United Nations, in which he said that the United States would be very happy to provide a training center and to try and establish a school for training United Nations staffers, is a very necessary thing and I applaud that. I hope that the United States goes forward with that.

One final comment. Cambodia has three to four million mines in it. One of the essential things that you need to teach people is to watch where they step. We lost a number of Bangladeshis out of the UNTAC mission almost every other day. I was putting Cambodian civilians in my Nissan and rushing them to the nearest medical facilities because they had stepped on mines. It is a horrible problem. All sides have been planting mines for 20 years. You can no longer assume that just because an area is a nice grassy knoll, there aren't mines underneath that grass. Secondary growth also impedes mine clearing operations. Mine clearing is absolutely critical, and mine awareness is even more so.

GENERAL DISCUSSION

THE CHAIR: I do want to just put a little note of balance here. There is a certain tone, suggesting we are beating up on the UN. This was not the purpose of the presentations made, But I think even those who are here from the UN would probably admit that there is a reform process underway and that it is needed. Fair enough. The Institute for National Strategic Studies is interested in what the United States needs to do to improve its own performance, to contribute better and to make UN peacekeeping or peace enforcement or Level-Two or Level-Three more

effective. I think those of you who have read Chairman Powell's
comments know his preference. I do not want to misquote him,
but certainly we learn in our United States schools the need for
overwhelming force for achieving decisive results. We have a
cultural problem, I would submit, in terms of adjusting the
manner in which we operate to be more effective in this sort of
political-military environment. I would foresee us doing more in
the future.

QUESTION: I am from the Department of Peacekeeping
Operations, so it has been very interesting for me to listen to the
discussions. I am responsible, among other things, for training
in the United Nations. The issue has been raised a number of
times—that training is very essential for future
peacekeepers—and I agree with that. But let me offer some
additional points. When we talk about United Nations
peacekeeping, we are talking about United Nations' operations.
In fact the operational issue in a country is rather limited,
because when the forces are there, what are we going to do? We
are dealing with supervision, monitoring, escorting, etc. In fact,
what we need is planning for the deployment of the force. The
logistical planning is essential for us— indeed, it is crucial. The
other point I would mention is the standby forces. When we are
talking about standby forces, it depends on the contributors. If
I am talking about standby forces from Sweden, it means
something else for me than if you're talking about standby forces
from the United States. We have standby forces within the
Nordic community dealing with peacekeeping that can be made
available within 14 days. But, in the US, we are talking about
24 hours, 48 hours or 72 hours. I think also the culture of
various countries differs quite a lot. If we have infantry battalion
from a country somewhere other than Western Europe, and we
have an infantry battalion from the Western Europe, there is a
difference.

   I think it is important for us within the UN to think about
how standby forces can reach a certain operational level. It
means for infantry battalions saying they have to do the
following things: equipment attached to the battalion,
communication equipment, vehicles, and units must be
self-contained for approximately two weeks. It is very difficult

for us to get these kinds of units today. It is easy for us to get units if they are coming just with the uniforms. But it is most important to get medical units and logistics units, air wings, the air transport and so on. I think we have to plan for what I call differing models of standby forces. This has implications for training. First, we can never confine training only to the military people. We need to provide training to the civilians, as well. Because we need to remember today peacekeeping forces are a combination of civilian and military components. One of the difficulties within existing peacekeeping operations,is that civilians do not always understand the military approach to an operation and vice versa. The other point is that we always say that we need to train the troop-contributing countries that are going to provide the United Nations with forces, but we have also to train the host country. It is important to train these people, to inform them of the objectives of peacekeeping the force. I do not know how many times I heard from one of the countries: "What is the purpose of the peacekeeping force? Is it an occupation force?" People do not understand peacekeeping forces are not a true military force. It is a military unit used in a political context. We cannot develop peacekeeping curricula for the United States and send it to Nigeria. But we can provide the nucleus, and they have to fill in the blanks. There are today several training institutions around the world dealing with peacekeeping. We have them in Europe, some in the Nordic countries, as has been mentioned. We have them in Austria, we have them in Poland, and we have Canada and Australia. And I think what we have to do, if not to unify the training, at least talk the same language.

Concerning new missions, you do not know what has been done so far when we talk about Somalia. We present training in two ways. First, what we do is to send to the advanced party in the country a disk with the training program. They have to alter the training program in accordance with the local conditions, because we are not sure about them up in the Headquarters. At the same time, the contingent's commanders, when they come to UN Headquarters, are briefed about the mission and at the same time they are briefed how to train their people. It is not necessary to train well-educated staff officers, battalion commanders, etc. The key persons in all the training, particularly in these kinds of peacekeeping operations we are dealing with today, are platoon and squad leaders because they have to take the most difficult decisions in the field. There are six videos in development. These videos deal with training. The point was that we found out a lot of countries know nothing about peacekeeping and even less about training. The first video deals with the causes and roots of a conflict; the second deals with the historical evolution of peacekeeping; the third deals with how you can use an original center for training; the fourth, with how to train the UN soldier; the fifth, with how to train a UN observer; the sixth, with how to train an election monitor. Hopefully, these six videos will have been completed by the end of the year, and we can get some money to have them translated into French and Spanish. As you can see, training is very essential for us, and I think we have done something to enhance it.

CHAIR: Thank you very much for your comments. I might just ask the panel whether they might wish to respond.

RESPONSE: Again, in a context of a balanced perspective, I would like to make the point, my remarks might have sounded like UN bashing, but it is not. What I felt I did in Central America was the most positive thing I have done in my life, bar none. From getting people like Dr. Ortega together with Commandante Franklin, to get them working on a peace process, to demobilizing an entire army, to destroying 20-odd-thousand weapons. It was very positive and it could not have happened without the United Nations. Your point on the military component, what seems to be missing is what we in the military see as essential in any of these operations as we go from Level-One to -Two to -Three; you must have those principles of unity of command which is not necessarily there. And when you get to a sort of Level One operation, perhaps such as the elections in Haiti and what have you, where the military commander was subordinate to the mission commander, fair enough. But when you go above that to Level-Two and -Three, unity of military command must be present, or we're going to lose soldiers and lose the operation. Your point on training is well taken. Senior officers training, staff officers training, are essential. We think we can handle this in the context of our normal officer development training, and we must do it. We Canadians haven't done it terribly well, but we are improving upon it. Your observer training especially, a thing which must be done for a week or two weeks depending on the background of the officer and the mission, that also has to be done. We do not see the requirement for a Canadian peacekeeping academy, which is being pushed by some people in Canada. I see us continuing to participate in the higher level academy learning for would-be chiefs of staff, force commanders and that sort of thing. It is quite important. If, indeed, in the case of the United States, it is required to make a political statement to underscore the point that a peacekeeping academy or a special organization is required, I certainly would understand that. But I do not think with the professionalism that exists in the United States Army as I know it you need a special peacekeeping academy.

SECOND RESPONSE: I wouldn't disagree, but there is just something I would like to add. One of the problems the UN faces is getting forces into the field quickly. One of the real problems, of course, is not only getting the military into the field, but getting the UN in the position to where it can second its military staff so that it begins to perform essential headquarter staff functions. One of the problems with the UN having 12 missions currently in the field—soon to be 13, of which two of those missions are the second and third largest ever mounted—the reality is that the United Nations has diluted its expertise in many of it's specialized logistics areas in the Secretariat because it was required to send it's experts to the field. There is great sense, in my view, to rotating key staff from various countries through all of the positions in the United Nations Secretariat dealing with peacekeeping. Whether it be finance, logistics, or operations, it makes sense to me that all of us provide people. I think many of us are willing to do so.

THIRD RESPONSE: I'd like to cover the civilian training side of the house. One of the problems we had was our civilian staff rotated too often. In the time I was in the field, we had three

chief procurement officers and four chief finance officers. You
cannot get any continuity as a result. A lot of these
folks—because the UN was stretched thin—were on their first
field assignment. They had no background training on the area
whatsoever. Complicating that was what was mentioned earlier
about unity of command. I know the UN is not a military
organization, but they need to establish clearly, who is in charge.
When you have a situation as we had in the Western Sahara
where the military forces were doing their thing, all those other
support groups existed only on paper. George [Stueber] talked
about the problems with police. We had no problems. We had
a police chief who was the chief of nothing. He was there all by
himself. Then we had an assistant special representative who was
resident for two weeks, then he went to train up the new special
representative.

From a military perspective, the senior man was our force
commander. But the civilians look at that sort of thing in a
different way. When we went to a lower level acting force
commander, regular general level, we had an assistant special
representative who was roughly at the same pay grade and a chief
administrative officer who was just a little bit below that pay
grade—and no one really said who was in charge. Now I know
what UN wiring diagrams say and all that, but to try to explain
to some young military officers who are accustomed to knowing
who is in charge and who you go to if you have a problem is
difficult when the concept is "put all these guys in a room, lock
the door, and see who comes out on top." This is not a very
good way to run things. The civilians need to train, the military
need to train; and one of the things that needs to be in the
curriculum is how to deal with each other, how to use your
powers of persuasion rather than just giving an order and
expecting somebody to carry it out. Our force commander had a
policy: when new observers came in they would serve a
minimum of thirty days out on a team site before they would get
a job in the force or sector headquarters. I know you cannot
afford to do that when you're looking at a platoon leader who
gets a short notice requirement to go out and take a Kalashnikov
away from a 16 year old Cambodian teenager or something like
that, but we were in a different situation and planning was done
for us. We did our own staff training, or we would have been

very hard pressed to graduate from Level-One to a Level-Two operation largely because the political planning was based on the false assumption that political successes would be achieved.

FINAL RESPONSE: Two comments. First, on civil-military staff training. As currently configured, a military operation that has a military headquarters supported by a civilian staff is unworkable. It is unworkable for a couple of reasons. First, the civilians have different rules. They work until maybe noon Saturday and then they go home for Saturday and Sunday. When you are out in the field you need support 24 hours a day, seven days a week. Second, civilians do not know military "things". I had a secretary from Switzerland; she was just a sweet lady, but she didn't know about military vocabulary, about operations or anything else, and she was holding down what would have been a position for a master sergeant in an operations cell. There were operations that weren't planned in UNTAC because there was a lack of experience and expertise there. Third, let's say you start out at Level-One and things get nasty. How are you now going to deploy those civilians into a Level-Three operation? More importantly, they have absolutely no expertise running a Level-Three type operation. That needs to be cured at the UN Headquarters level, and it needs to be done quickly, because there are a lot of Level-Twos out there that could become nasty. The next question involves training. The training that I am advocating for staff is not to bring Canadians and US officers and other people up-to-speed on how to do staff work, because we already do a pretty good job on that. But when you are going to deploy a staff on a military operation, it is bad policy to get them on the ground where they meet for the first time. I would much rather have a place where once you have identified that you'll have a mission going out, you have identified what that mission is to accomplish and what they are allowed and not allowed to do. I would like to send them someplace—maybe Fort Dix—where I can give them simulation training so that they can work together as staff groups to produce the staff products required—the intelligence products, the logistics planning products, the operational product—before they get on the ground, and they have all the real life alligators biting them so that they do not know what they are doing. I think that's absolutely key. More importantly, I think this is an easy one to solve. Often you see that there are north-south antipathies. If you have a staff training school, that brings officers up to speed regarding good staff procedures, that is a professional carryover that can be used when they go back to their nations.

QUESTION: My question concerns MINURSO. I didn't actually go to MINURSO myself, but my colleague Jack Chopper who works with me did. And he did actually testify to the Senate and at the General Assembly on his findings. He has quite a story to tell. He visited the Polisario through Algeria,and he visited the Moroccan side at the request of the Norwegians after the caucus we had in Morocco. On the latter journey,he was arrested twice in the area, and he returned with the impression that the UN observers are a boxed-in force, comparatively speaking. He cites the fact that the hotels they live in are actually prescribed areas, and he wasn't able to enter them and tell that you lived on the Moroccan side because it is fenced off by the police. You cannot fly a UN flag. You have a fault with your violation reports which do not actually reach the percentage of actual reports that come into public scrutiny. It is vastly less than the number of violation reports that you wrote. So I have two questions. Are they really boxed in? Or is this our imagination? Do they really enjoy the freedom of movement which is granted to them under the mandate?

RESPONSE: I cannot speak for what has happened since I left the end of July, but you are right, we are somewhat boxed-in by one side of the conflict. I did not want to get into a "who shot John" comment, saying one side is cooperating with the United Nations and the other is not. Those kinds of comments have been raised to New York, and for whatever reason, we are still constrained by the Moroccans. It is true, they probably wouldn't let that fellow into the hotel. You see the Moroccans do not consider, what they call D-Day as having occurred yet. They treat the UN force there as being a guest. And for a guy like me from the United States I resented being monitored all the time, having people go through my hotel room while I'm at work. These sorts of issues have been raised to New York. What is being done about it, I do not know. We are moving just about everywhere we want to go except the Moroccans do not let us into their strong points along the berm, and the general who is in charge of those forces, told our force commander: "I will personally escort you into that strong point as soon as my king gives me permission to do so." Now, that's above the level of our military force to resolve. We also talked about the mine problem. Despite the fact that the Moroccans say that they are sharing minefield data with the UN Observer Force, we were pretty well convinced that we were not getting a lot of minefield data that they do have about the mines they put out, even though some of them may have shifted in the sands over the years. They are also not sharing information about the total disposition of their forces. These problems have all been made known to New York, but the perception of the observers on the ground is that there is not a whole lot of arm twisting going on back at the Security Council level.

I know it is very debilitating when you spend a lot of time preparing draft Secretary-General's reports for the military force inputs that talk about logistics problems and movement restrictions, and then the final product is a very watered down thing. The last one that came before I left didn't even contain the word logistics anywhere in the entire report. Which, to me, if I was an ambassador at the United Nations and I read this thing or sat in on Security Council deliberations trying to decide whether to approve that report or not, I would say: "Hey! things must be hunky dory in MINURSO." Yes, we are somewhat boxed in by one side over there. For whatever reason, and it is not as though we've accepted that and laid down and rolled over and said, "well that makes our job easier we do not have to do as much patrolling." We have tried to deal with that with some limited success. I do not know what the situation is at present.

ADDITIONAL COMMENT: The situation you describe is analogous to the situation in Cambodia. When we deployed one team to a site, they were kept under armed guard, virtual house arrest. They were allowed no contact with any of the Cambodians. They were never allowed into the headquarters of the Khmer Rouge. They have no idea if that is really the HQs for the KR; it most probably is not. They did not allow any UN helicopters into the area for two months. My team went into the area under the auspices of the "CIANOOK" faction and were told by the commander of the Khmer Rouge 616 division that he would kill me and my entire team. There was never any action taken by the United Nations concerning this incident. This goes back to my initial point. Before a mission goes in, the United Nations leadership needs to decide how they propose to achieve the mission's goal. What economic, political, and military pressure will they exert? And they also have to spell out what is failure. When do you cut your losses and say the organization is not going to be able to achieve the mission, and anything else we throw at it is a waste of resources? That again, has not been done. I raised those questions with General Sanderson early on in the mission when it was painfully obvious that the KR had no intention of cooperating with the peace agreement and before we had deployed 11 battalions and 15,000 people. Decisions on how to fulfill the mission and criteria for success and failure should have been made. So it goes back to the planning, the real concept of what the mission is going to achieve and how it will be achieved.

FURTHER RESPONSE: To substantiate the two examples that were made, you are always faced with this problem. We had them playing games with us and our freedom of movement, which was agreed to by all concerned but was not granted. We had to press, cajole, educate them, and finally over all protestations, take a militarily calculated risk to get into the Imales Valley, which was the home of the Contras, who didn't want us to go there. Anyway, when we came back we had complaints all over the place from the United States Embassy. Our mission was not in concert with what they wanted, but we pushed and made a military decision, and took a calculated risk which was described by some as being foolhardy. But once that was done and contact had been made, it all unfolded from there. You've got to keep pressing and that's where the military estimate process and the ability and the desire and the necessity of taking risks comes in.

THE CHAIR: Let me try briefly to indicate our conclusions for US military planners in signing up to a UN operation—whether it is level-One, Level-Two, level-Three, individual observer, small size unit, or large size unit.

First, well trained US units do not need a major reorientation of their training program in terms of predeployment training, but, they will need sensitivity training or cultural training to get them immersed in the social, cultural milieu into which they will deploy.

Second, you certainly have to know what kind of mission it is-whether it is Level-One, Two-, or Three-. Training alone is not going to satisfy Level Three. We probably need to buttress our approach to education about UN operations in our professional military education. We do a little bit of it at present, but I do not think we do it terribly well. We need to enhance it in the Command and General Staff College, because majors and lieutenant colonels are going to be out there doing the job as individual observers or whatever. We must do it at the War Colleges, as well, because their graduates may be the force commanders or key staff officers, etc. I believe it was General Douglas who mentioned the importance of reconnaissance. The UN technical surveys should be done jointly. The nations that are going to participate should go on the technical survey with the UN officials, so that there are no unresolved issues between the nations that are going to contribute forces and the UN.

We, the United States, want to make sure that we have this reservoir of skills and talent. I know the Army does it in the FAO program, but we need to make sure all the Services are developing a similar reservoir. As a result, we will know who we've got, where they've been, whether they can be called on again, etc. But, it has to contribute to a person's career. And that probably means the United States military has to go through a little acculturation. Participation in peacekeeping operations should be rewarded and should contribute to a one's career. If we say that, but do not do it, nobody's going to want to sign up for a peacekeeping mission.

As to selection of people for peacekeeping missions, I do not know whether you need a psychological profile, but I can see some situations as very stressful, which means that you've got to have the right person there. I am also struck by the need for a professional UN staff officers' course. I think our President suggested that in his speech. Personally, I think we can build on the approach.

The UN Contribution to International Security

Ambassador Thomas R. Pickering
US Permanent Representative
to the United Nations

THE FUTURE SECURITY ROLE of the UN is, to put it mildly, a speculative topic. In reality it requires three separate forecasts: one, about the dominant security concerns of the coming years; another concerning the use of multilateral security tools relative to regional or unilateral ones; and a third regarding the specific contributions the UN might make.

Triple forecasts are better assignments for futures traders and risk averse diplomats, for whom the act of speculation always quickens the pulse. But when, as now, the world is in upheaval, you need a certain amount of speculation just to get to the end of each day. Unfortunately today it looks like I will be starting early. With that comment I will venture some thoughts on the very intriguing subject you have chosen, with the understanding they will be treated as personal musings with no official status.

US SECURITY INTERESTS AFTER THE COLD WAR

Over the last two years it has grown increasingly evident that the end of the Cold War removed from the international political system its central organizing principle. In his speech to the General Assembly last month, and in statements prompted by Iraq's invasion of Kuwait and the UN's response, President Bush offered a replacement. The essence of the President's vision is a New World Order. He has described   it in the following words:

> The New World Order does not mean surrendering our sovereignty or forfeiting our interests. It really describes a responsibility imposed by our successes. It refers to new ways of working with other nations to deter aggression and to achieve stability, to achieve prosperity and, above all, to achieve peace. It springs from hopes for a world based on a shared commit ment to a set of principles that undergird our relations - peaceful   settlement of disputes,

solidarity against aggression, reduced and controlled arsenals, and just treatment of peoples.

What are the security implications of a transition from the Cold War to the kind of New World Order the President has described? If one looks at US post-Cold War security interests through a UN window one way to describe the view is to talk about two adjacent circles separated by a rather permeable border.   In the first circle are core US security interests: protection against direct attack; protection of US citizens abroad; aid and support of allies; maintenance of unmolested international communications and commerce; assurance of access to vital resources; insulation of essential interests from the effects of foreign wars - such as the tanker escorts late in the Iran-Iraq War; and so on.

In the second circle are the general and broad goals, values and principles which are the essence of that civil international society whose vision President Bush invokes by speaking of a New World Order or a "Pax Universalis". It embraces the rule of law, non-aggression and the pacific settlement of disputes, respect for sovereignty, defense of human rights, control of arsenals, curbs on proliferation and in general a disciplined, cooperative approach to common security. This morning I want to explore a narrow but extremely important question at the heart of the UN's role in strengthening and enforcing those principles, that is, the UN authorized use of force.

MULTILATERAL VS. REGIONAL USE OF FORCE

As a point of departure let me say that the centrality of the UN Security Council to the shaping and legitimizing of the response to Iraqi aggression has raised expectations, hence political pressure, for a comparable Council role in other crises. Expectations that the UN will swiftly act on the Haitian coup, the civil wars in Yugoslavia, and in Liberia last year, illustrate the point. In many such crises, UN action may indeed be appropriate and helpful (particularly where, as in Haiti, its prior involvement clearly makes it an interested party. But the larger point is that the Charter never intended the Security Council to be its only or full time court of first resort. Indeed, Article 52 explicitly mandates regional efforts to resolve or redress threats to peace and security before resort to the UN. And that is a good thing. The forceful and immediate OAS response to the overthrow of the Aristide government in Haiti, and the constructive engagement of the EC and CSCE in the Yugoslav situation, suggest cohesion and solidarity   arising from shared regional, political and cultural interests permit a wider scope for action. Even in Liberia, where the ECOWAS effort to bring peace has not been aided by regional Anglophone-Francophone divisions, the recent Yamasoukro III agreement is a major step toward ending hostilities and bringing new elections.

Having said that, it is best to remember that none of these situations is resolved and the future is likely to bring crises that are not regionally containable, reinforcing the need for a selective approach to Security Council crisis management. One value of regional groups in this respect is that their greater willingness to act eventually bolsters the Security Council's role at such time as it may become necessary.

One of the things that drives this global/regional question is the character of conflict itself. Readers of the daily summaries prepared by the intelligence community know that most entries describe conflicts within states not between them. In the post Desert Storm period that is an instructive fact. It reminds us that threats to regional stability will not result primarily from the miscalculations of expansionist powers. As the Middle East and Yugoslavia daily demonstrate, regional stability after the Cold War--as it was before it--is largely shaped by essentially parochial concerns of an ethnic, religious, political, economic and social character. This may cause some nostalgia about the neatness and clarity of the Iraqi threat, which from both a political and a strategic perspective was more a caricature of the Cold War with a legal overlay and an ostentatious villain than a useful metaphor for the untidy challenges and conflicts ahead.

A daily dilemma facing the UN's security rule in this context is that, while the rule of law and the role of order are more comfortably complementary after the Cold War, they are not equivalent. Our humanitarian and political interest in seeing an orderly resolution in Yugoslavia may not conflict with, but it certainly exceeds any responsibilities conferred by relevant

international law. Similarly, international law has little positive
and nothing dispositive to say about the responsibilities of other
states in the event of coups and anarchy or bloodshed within a
neighbor's borders except to the extent that a potential for
spillover arises. In fact the rule of law would permit-though it is
unpleasant to ponder - a world convulsed by extraordinarily
destructive but utterly legal conflict. (The OAS Santiago
Declaration about the non-acceptability of governmental change
by coup represents an important exception and step forward
DOW under test in Haiti).

This dilemma is not helped by the fact that the common law
of states as well as the covenants and treaties agreed between
them permit competing and conflicting claims. Nowhere is this
more evident than when the international community is forced to
choose between the rights of states and the rights of peoples. As
you know, Security Council resolution 678 authorized action to
enforce Article 2 of the UN Charter's prohibition against the use
of force against another state. As you also know, resolution 688
found that persecution of Iraqi Kurds posed a danger to
international peace and security, a finding which in the majority
s view superseded another principle of the same Article
(paragraph 7), prohibiting intervention in the domestic affairs
of member states.

Yet the fact that 688 was very difficult to negotiate,
notwithstanding both the genocidal issues and the presence of
the "spillover threat" effect, and the subsequent resistance to very
forceful resolutions on Yugoslavia and Haiti suggests two things
to me. First, there is work to do before the Security Council is
ready regularly to serve as global crisis manager, much less
tribune of the New World Order; and second, that we must
remain open to alternative regional and even unilateral tools to
serve the "order" as well as the "law and justice" agendas
expressed by the President.

In a sense this approach to security leads us back to first
principles. Part of the "work" we have to do is the same that
our membership in the UN and other international institutions has
always required. It is the toilsome task of nurturing an
international society of common values, to inform and vitalize the
orderly world the President calls for and which we all wish to
live in. Civil order in the US benefits from the absorptive power

of shared values and a common culture which can dull differences, lessen rivalries and make most of us stake-holders in the status quo.

The absence of a parallel culture internationally, however tolerable during the Cold War, is now a source of frustration, as attested by the Council's recent failure to adopt a strong resolution calling for the restoration of Haitian democracy out of concern for the non-intervention doctrine in the hemisphere. While the collapse of communism has eliminated the major global clash of values it has had an opposite effect on other nationalist, tribal, religious, economic and ethnic conflicts that have been there for some time and may even reenergize North-South economic discord. For this reason, we are unlikely to see the rapid elaboration of international law or Security Council practice to provide assured external guarantees for minority rights, democratically elected governments, or hungry people caught in a civil war when a significant number of Council members do not see such principles as leading to order but subversive of it, at least subversive of an order based on firm doctrines of state sovereignty and non- intervention.

For an evolving but ambitious global security system I think the answer to this problem is to be pragmatic: that is, we try to bridge the gap between "order" and "law" when we can: we seek to fill it in on the infrequent occasions when that is possible; and when neither approach suffices, we look outside the UN for another forum or tool. Let me give an example of each approach. For the first response, the case of the Kurds and resolution 688 points in the right direction. The resolution did not explicitly mandate Operation Provide Comfort. Instead, it declared that the situation constituted a threat to international peace and security and called for member states to give assistance to the Secretary General's humanitarian efforts. With these two elements and the fact that Iraq was a country already under subject to Chapter VII enforcement, 688 was enough to open a legal space for the coalition to provide relief and support for the Kurds, a space which was not challenged by those Permanent and other Council Members   otherwise opposed to a more frontal approach on non-intervention grounds.

Regarding the second approach - bridging the gap between

the wider goals of a New World Order and the more modest requirements of current international law - a very helpful start would be early Congressional ratification of the International Covenant of Legal and Political Rights. Given the very large number of signatories already, United States accession to that treaty would strengthen the standing of the democratic, civil and minority rights embodied in it. A similar but possibly more difficult undertaking would be to examine ways to strengthen such weaknesses in international humanitarian law as the rights of afflicted peoples for access to humanitarian relief during wartime.

On this question of norm-building and its relation to security it is revealing to look again at regional organizations. For example, the OAS now has a legal instrument authorizing strong action, including use of economic and diplomatic sanctions, to reverse coups against democratically elected governments. Of course, the UN lacks anything comparable, but so does the CSCE s Paris Charter, the EC's Rome Treaty, the Western European Union's Charter nor even NATO. Yet the notable thing about Europe is that failure to agree on a security identity has not prevented it from acting in an increasingly coherent, increasingly forceful way towards Yugoslavia. The "watch what we do not what we say" quality of Europe on Yugoslavia, and the Security Council on Iraq and to a lesser extent the OAS on Haiti all leads to the not very surprising discovery that in the development of new security system, necessity is the primary mother of invention.

The third response to the limitations of the UN is to understand when it may still be necessary to bypass it. Neither the exercise of our rights under Article 51, of careful engagement in support of the principles of the New World Order require us to act under explicit UN authority. Nor is it difficult to imagine circumstances where either the fast-breaking nature of the threat or the inability of the Security Council to reach a decision argue for rapid unilateral or regional action.

Nonetheless, the Security Council now has a more credible and central status. We have done much to bring this about. We have done so in the belief that in the post-Cold War world, given the marginal nature of most threats to our wider environment, we have a great deal to gain from an effective and influential

Security Council. It strikes me then that we should strive to shape our policies and their expression to protect that investment.

With the exception of the Korean War, the subject of UN authorized enforcement actions and their legal and practical features is an unwritten text. Nor is the job of writing that text aided by the fact that the threats we must deal with fit awkwardly into any imaginable UN based structure. And neither will the UN - however strengthened - easily embrace the potentially wide security mission of a New World Order. So we should look to the UN to deliver a part of the solution at best. The regional organizations will add their part, backed up by the Security Council if necessary. And we must, as I have noted, keep open the door when necessary for national actions.

On the other hand, two key elements of a new approach to security will be legitimacy and flexibility, assets robustly developed by the UN in its management of the Iraqi challenge.

"LEGITIMACY" AND THE USE OF FORCE

As a starting point, we need to understand what constitutes "legitimacy" for an armed action hoping to secure its political flank. For ourselves and our allies, Resolution 678 authorizing "all necessary means" to secure Iraq's immediate and unconditional withdrawal, was close to an ideal formulation. It gave a UN license for the use of force without restriction as to its manner or extent, or terms for its cessation ,both important military and political considerations.

Not surprisingly these same attributes gave discomfort to many other UN members. The Secretary General himself has commented that while the war against Iraq was "made legitimate by the Security Council" it "was not a UN victory" since that could have resulted only from "hostilities controlled and directed by the UN". One need not share Perez de Cuellar's view to appreciate his point: the most iron- clad legal justification may not buy us that more evanescent political commodity called legitimacy. For example, the ambiguity of the phrase "all necessary means" meant that actions necessary for Desert Storm's success might in the view of the Council majority have exceeded the intent of 678. While that did not occur it created an uncovered risk. Another consideration is that broadly licensing a few countries to use force in the Council's name enables detractors to argue that the action is the project of a few governments unrepresentative of the world community.

For military action comparable in scale to Desert Storm, there does not seem an obvious answer to this problem since any significant degree of UN direction and control could have imposed disabling constraints. On the other hand, we hope and believe that the scale of Iraq-Kuwait is unlikely to be repeated in the foreseeable future, nor are immediate US interests likely to be so directly and vitally engaged. Moreover, Council cohesion nurtured by the Iraq experience could carry over to other issues. If this proves true, there may be scope for enhancing the Security Council's role in future peace enforcement.

ARTICLE 43 AGREEMENTS

One way the Charter offers to do that is by negotiation of Article 43 agreements between the Security Council and countries it selects. Paragraph I of Article 43 quests member states to:

> Undertake to make available to the Security Council, on its call, and in accordance with a special agreement or agreements, armed forces, assistance and facilities, including right of passage, necessary for the purpose of maintaining peace and security.

My own reading of Article 43 suggests several relevant points:

First, the conclusion of such an agreement need not confer an automatic, mandatory obligation to provide troops to the Security Council, but could instead simply state their availability subject to certain terms or procedures.

Second, Article 43 is silent on command arrangements: the phrase "on its call" does not necessarily mean "at its direction."

Third, by specifying "assistance and facilities" the language permits members to satisfy their obligations by means other than provision of combat troops - a useful flexibility.

Fourth, paragraph 3 specifies that agreements shall be at the initiative of the Security Council, a helpful limiting factor that ensures selectivity.

Finally, paragraph 3 also states that agreements may be between the Council and individual members or groups of members, offering a potential basis for associations between the Security Council and regionally based alliances. Since alliances offer a more functional basis for concerted military action than a chance grouping of UN member states, this too could be a useful feature.

DELEGATION OF ENFORCEMENT

A vital question about '43' is whether, and what kind, of command arrangements it implies. In my view 43 agreements are not incompatible with signatories exercise of wide military latitude when those agreements are invoked. In this sense that agreement might be less a format for direct Council control than an expression of its general capacity to enforce decisions and hence a means of deterrence. In fact, agreements with powerful members or groups of members might have a psychological impact similar to a classic mutual assistance pact, strengthening respect for decision under Articles 39 (power of recommendation), 40 (provisional measures) and 41 (embargoes, diplomatic and other sanctions) and by extension, for statements of the Secretary General or the Council President. On the other hand of course, the reality of the Permanent Member veto would remain a factor in this as in any other effort to extend the Council's scope.

As we consider different approaches to the UN we need to bear in mind that the notion of such delegated enforcement is not alien to the Charter but explicitly anticipated in three places. Article 48 empowers the Council to determine which members shall conduct the action required to carry out its decisions "for the maintenance of international peace and security". Article 53 permits the Council to utilize "regional arrangements or agencies for enforcement action under its authority". Finally, Article 106 authorizes the victorious World War II allies to consult with a view to joint action necessary to maintain peace and security, although as a practical matter 106 is widely regarded as an outdated anachronism and an effort to revive it would be both impractical and divisive.

SECURITY COUNCIL OVERSIGHT OF MILITARY ACTION

Notwithstanding the legality of delegated enforcement, we should allow for the possibility that the Council will not absent itself so completely from command and control as it did in resolution 678. As you know, Chapter VII provides vehicles for Council involvement:

> Article 42 permits it to act by air, sea or land forces to give effect to its decisions when Article 41 measures are deemed inadequate;

> Article 46 calls for the Council to develop plans for the application of armed force with the assistance of a Military Staff Committee (MSC);

> Article 47 details the MSC's terms of reference, which include advice to the Council on arms control, readiness planning, general matters of command as well as strategic direction of forces.

Any move in this direction will raise concerns among troop contributors. The chapter's emphasis on the MSC is especially problematic: no state whose troops are engaged in hostilities is likely to allow their direction by a group to which it does not belong or whose members have necessarily also contributed troops. This is also the need to ensure that committed troops are not subject to life-threatening surprises by changes in the political parameters governing their use, or by a breach in security or by other factors arising from activities which might be implied by the words "strategic direction". Thirdly, unless the reference to strategic command (47.3) is interpreted in some static sense, the technology of modem warfare probably makes it obsolete: it requires flexible, decentralized decisionmaking and instantaneous communication - neither is well suited to decision by UN committee.

Yet there may by ways of partially employing Articles 42 and 47 while inoculating them against their most intrusive potential and these may be worth exploring particularly in the context of small scale or low intensity conflict. For example, a more explicit articulation of war aims may sometimes be desirable. More specific goals do not mean more modest one, but they do make the Security Council more accountable for actions to secure them. A war aims statement might also specify minimum terms for cessation of hostilities - as distinct from terms for an overall settlement.   A general statement of permissible means would add legitimacy by further distinguishing peace enforcement from other use of force, though such pronouncements would only be advisable to the extent they did not expose troops to additional risk.   We may also wish to explore arrangements whereby peace enforcers could report regularly and in person to the Council itself or a sub-group of the Council.   While not altering command relationships, such a consultative link could be a helpful tool for preserving consensus.

THE UN AND COALITION FORCES

One of the questions our security community will need to consider is the issue of command and operational integration of the forces which might be employed to give effect to a Security Council decision.   This requires a trade-off between the need to avoid over-identification with a few countries, and the exigencies of the unity of command, rapid deployment, coordinated movements, and so on.   Before going beyond the level of joint action employed in Desert Storm, in many substantive respects a NATO operation, are we persuaded that there are militarily and politically satisfactory answers to many unanalyzed questions about non-NATO coalition warfare? It was this sort of appreciation for the unexpected that prompted this comment from George C. Marshall in 1938:

With us, geographical location and the international situation make
it literally impossible to find definite answers for such questions as:
Who will be our enemy in the next war; in what theater of
operations will it be fought; and what will be our national objective
at the time?

But today's planners have a tougher task: not only do we not
know the identity of our future adversaries, neither do we
necessarily know who are our friends--in the sense of coalition
partners--will be. Yet joint arrangements for defeating a capable
foe will require substantial unity of command and control, and
the standard peacekeeping command format--decentralized
command across national sectors--may not suffice under the
fluidity of combat conditions. A technologically advanced but
weakly united UN force might even be at a disadvantage against
a low-tech but well directed opponent.   Such considerations
suggest that a significant level of interoperability may be needed
for UN-authorized military operations. Between forces of vastly
differing capabilities with no history of cooperations, which
would seem to require achieving a sort of "UN standard"
paralleling that of peacekeeping.   It could involve such things as
doctrine, rules of engagement, training and joint exercises,
command and control, IFF systems, intel-sharing, language;
logistic support and so on. Achieving all of this would mean
unheard of levels of military openness and may be difficult for
governments to accept outside an alliance context. A further
detailed look at most of these issues in house would be a useful
beginning step to help flesh out the contours of the new order we
seek.

ENHANCING PREVENTIVE DIPLOMACY

At your request, these remarks have focussed on the use-of-force
aspects of the UN's security roles. Let me conclude by returning
to more familiar ground: The UN and conflict avoidance. In the
communique of the London Summit the G7 leaders committed
themselves to shoring up the basis for UN preventive diplomacy--
a theme the President revisited when he addressed the General

Assembly last month.

To fulfill this goal the institution will need to shift to a higher gear. Useful steps could include:

1.   Informal information sharing, by ourselves and other member states, to keep the Secretary General fully informed of existing or potential situations which could lead to international friction; (this is now occurring within the context of resolution 687's Iraqi NMD inspection program).

2.   Requiring disputants or potential disputants to keep the Secretary General and through him the Security Council, fully informed of all pertinent facts;

3.   Supporting the enhanced use of special representatives in good offices and quiet diplomacy missions to help resolve issues which may lead to conflict;

4.   And finally, inviting the Secretary General and the Council to give early consideration to the use of UN forces as a means of forestalling conflict before hostilities occur, such as by deployment to the borders of a threatened state. This may well involve elements of traditional peacekeeping and of peace enforcement as well.

On the subject of peacekeeping itself, as you know we are in a major growth phase. The UN has undertaken more missions in the last three years than in its first 43. The scope and variety of functions has grown as will.   It is time to strengthen the organized structure of peacekeeping planning and management in order to keep up with the heavier workload.

It is also time to put peacekeeping financing on a more stable longterm footing commensurate with its importance to global security--and our won. A step in the right direction within the US would be to take a hard look now at creating a substantial peacekeeping account possibly within, or in relationship to, the Department of Defense budget, in recognition of the clear security purposes of peacekeeping expenditure.

CONCLUSION

From time to time as history turns remarkable corners, writers use the term "annus mirabilis", or "miraculous year" to express their amazement. These are indeed amazing times. They are not, however, from a security point of view, miraculous. There is no shortage of causes which human beings will kill or die for. Nor will we now retire all of the classic tools for pursuing and defending our interests. Nor will others. But I would submit that the UN's capacity to serve common security concerns has never been greater nor more susceptible to constructive thinking or influence.

McNair Papers

The McNair Papers are published at Fort Lesley J. McNair, home of the Institute for National Strategic Studies and the National Defense University. An Army post since 1794, the fort was given its present name in 1948 in honor of Lieutenant General Lesley James McNair. General McNair, known as "Educator of the Army" and trainer of some three million troops, was about to take command of Allied ground forces in Europe under Eisenhower, when he was killed in combat in Normandy, 25 July 1944.

1. Joseph P. Lorenz, *Egypt and the New Arab Coalition*, February 1989.
2. John E. Endicott, *Grand Strategy and the Pacific Region*, May 1989.
3. Eugene V. Rostow, *President, Prime Minister, or Constitutional Monarch?*, October 1989.
4. Howard G. DeWolf, *SDI and Arms Control*, November 1989.
5. Martin C. Libicki, *What Makes Industries Strategic*, November 1989.
6. Melvin A. Goodman, *Gorbachev and Soviet Policy in the Third World*, February 1990.
7. John Van Oudenaren, "The Tradition of Change in Soviet Foreign Policy," and Francis Conte, "Two Schools of Soviet Diplomacy," in *Understanding Soviet Foreign Policy*, April 1990.
8. Max G. Manwaring and Court Prisk, *A Strategic View of Insurgencies: Insights from El Salvador*, May 1990.
9. Steven R. Linke, *Managing Crises in Defense Industry: The PEPCON and Avtex Cases*, June 1990.
10. Christine M. Helms, *Arabism and Islam: Stateless Nations and Nationless States*, September 1990.
11. Ralph A. Cossa, *Iran: Soviet Interests, US Concerns*, July 1990.
12. Ewan Jamieson, *Friend or Ally? A Question for New Zealand*, May 1991.
13. Richard J. Dunn III, *From Gettysburg to the Gulf and Beyond: Coping with Revolutionary Technological Change in Land Warfare*,
14. Ted Greenwood, *U.S. and NATO Force Structure and Military*

Operations in the Mediterranean, June 1993.

15. Oscar W. Clyatt, Jr., *Bulgaria's Quest for Security After the Cold War*, February 1993.

16. William C. Bodie, *Moscow's "Near Abroad": Security Policy in Post-Soviet Europe*, June 1993.

17. William H. Lewis (ed.), *Military Implications of United Nations Peacekeeping Operations*, June 1993.

18. Sterling D. Sessions and Carl R. Jones, *Interoperability: A Desert Storm Case Study*, July 1993.

19. Eugene V. Rostow, *Should Article 43 of the United Nations Charter Be Raised From the Dead?* July 1993

20. William T. Johnsen and Thomas Durell-Young; Jeffrey Simon; Daniel N. Nelson; William C. Bodie, and James McCarthy, *European Security Toward the Year 2000,* August 1993.

21. Edwin R. Carlisle, ed., *Developing Battlefield Technologies in the 1990s*, August 1993.

22. Patrick Clawson, *How Has Saddam Hussein Survived? Economic Sanctions, 1990–93*, August 1993.

ISBN 0-16-041972-7

90000

9 780160 419720